Essential Histories

The Spanish Invasion of Mexico
1519–1521

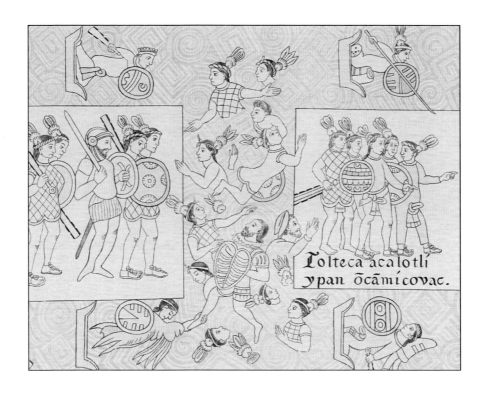

Ɫolteca acalotlí
ypan ōcāmicovac.

Essential Histories

The Spanish Invasion of
Mexico 1519–1521

Charles M Robinson III

First published in Great Britain in 2004 by Osprey Publishing,
Midland House, West Way, Botley, Oxford OX2 0PH, UK
44-02 23rd St, Suite 219, Long Island City, NY 11101, USA
E-mail: info@ospreypublishing.com

Transferred to digital print on demand 2009

First published 2004
1st impression 2004

Printed and bound by PrintOnDemand-Worldwide.com, Peterborough, UK

A CIP catalogue record for this book is available from the British Library

ISBN: 978 1 84176 563 1

Editorial by Judith Millidge
Design by Ken Vail Graphic Design, Cambridge, UK
Index by Alan Thatcher
Cartography by The Map Studio
Picture research by Image Select International
Origination by Grasmere Digital Imaging, Leeds, UK
Typeset in Monotype Gill Sans and ITC Stone Serif

Author's Note

Unlike the various Maya dialects, the Nahuatl language of Aztec Mexico was first written down by Spanish priests following the
Conquest. The early conquistadors either took the words down as they heard them, or depended on the translations of the native girl
known to history as doña Marina, who spoke a different dialect to that used in Mexico proper. Consequently, many Nahuatl words and
names were misspelled. Among others, Motecuhçoma eventually came to be rendered as Montezuma, and Cuauhtémoc became
Guatemoc or Guatemotzin (the suffix –tzin meaning "lord"). Except for direct quotes, I have used the spellings preferred in modern
Mexico.

At the time of the Conquest, the terms "Mexico" and "Mexican" pertained exclusively to the region under immediate Aztec suzerainty,
which is to say the modern Federal District (Mexico City and environs) and the adjacent State of Mexico (a separate state within the
Mexican Republic), rather than the area of the present Mexican Republic. The word "Aztec" was obsolete by 1519, was not
resurrected until the 18th century, and was probably not in common usage until the publication of William Hickling Prescott's *History of
the Conquest of Mexico* in 1843. Consequently, the contemporary accounts use "Mexico" and "Mexican", the Castilians not having
heard "Aztec."

Most of the men in Cortés's army were from Castile, the dominant kingdom of Spain. They were divided into those from Castile proper
and those from the outlying province of Extremadura, the homeland of Cortés. For simplicity, the soldiers of Cortés's original band will
be referred to collectively as they generally referred to themselves, as Castilians.

In the decades following Christopher Columbus's first voyage, West Indian words worked their way into common usage among the
Spaniards living in the Indies, and were included in the conversations and writings of the Europeans about the Conquest. Therefore, in
primary Spanish sources, one often finds the Cuban *cúe* (temple) and *cacique* (lord or chief), rather than their Castilian or
Nahuatl equivalents.

FOR A CATALOGUE OF ALL BOOKS PUBLISHED BY OSPREY
MILITARY AND AVIATION PLEASE CONTACT:

Osprey Direct, c/o Random House Distribution Center,
400 Hahn Road, Westminster, MD 21157
Email: uscustomerservice@ospreypublishing.com

Osprey Direct, The Book Service Ltd, Distribution Centre,
Colchester Road, Frating Green, Colchester, Essex, CO7 7DW
E-mail: customerservice@ospreypublishing.com

www.ospreypublishing.com

Contents

Introduction

In the spring of 1519, some 600 adventurers led by Hernán Cortés, a failed law student-turned planter and speculator, embarked on the conquest of a ruthless and predatory empire with an army numbering in the tens of thousands. The Spanish conquest of Mexico was the greatest military expedition in history, and in achieving it, Cortés proved himself one of the foremost generals of all time.

The Conquest completely changed the history of the world. The establishment of a European power on the mainland of the western hemisphere opened the door for a complete European hegemony, ultimately leading to the establishment of independent states. Whether this was for better or worse is a question for the philosophers. The fact is that it did happen, and now, some 500 years later, a western hemisphere nation is the dominant power in the world. And while the United States may be the cultural heir to Great Britain, to a large extent it has inherited civilizing influences from Spain, too: fully one-third of the nation was once a part of "New Spain", as the Spaniards came to call Mexico. San Antonio, Texas, Santa Fe, New Mexico, and Monterey, California, were all seats of Spanish government until 1821, and of Mexican government until even later, and Spanish and English are spoken side by side throughout the American southwest. This is the legacy of Hernán Cortés and his conquistadors.

Chronology

In studying the Conquest, one finds different dates for the same events, depending on the publication. The conquistadors themselves used the Julian calendar which, among other things, assigned additional days to February. By the early 16th century, it was about ten days behind the modern calendar. Thus the date of Cuauhtémoc's surrender, given as August 13 1519, actually would have been August 23. Roman Catholic countries, such as Spain, adopted the more accurate Gregorian calendar in 1582, but the old accounts were not updated. Consequently, while many modern authors continue to use the dates recorded by the conquistadors, others try to convert them. For the sake of simplicity, and to conform with the majority of works, I have stayed with the Julian system. Occasionally, there are discrepancies. For example, Bernal Díaz, writing from memory in old age, dates the launching of the brigantines to blockade the city to May 26 1521, while Cortés, writing within months of the event, places it on April 28. In such cases, I have used the source written nearest to the event.

1517
February–April Francisco Hernández de Córdoba explores Yucatán and Campeche, suffering heavy losses in battle with the organized Indian kingdoms.

1518
January–October Juan de Grijalva explores the Yucatán and Mexican coasts, trades with local city-states, and learns of the Aztec empire.
October 23 Cuban governor Diego Velásquez commissions Hernán Cortés to lead a third expedition.
November 18 Cortés sails from Santiago de Cuba, in defiance of the governor. Finishes fitting out at Trinidad and San Cristóbal de la Habana.

1519
February 10 Cortés sails for Mexico, arriving a few days later in Cozumel.
March 14 Departure from Cozumel.
March 22–23 After sailing around Yucatán, Cortés lands in Tabasco, meeting resistance from the natives.
March 25 Annunciation Day. Cortés takes the town of Potonchán. doña Marina joins the expedition.
April 18 Palm Sunday. Expedition departs from Tabasco.
April 21 Maundy Thursday. Fleet arrives off San Juan Ulúa, outside modern harbor of Veracruz. Castilians found Villa Rica de la Vera Cruz.
Good Friday Cortés goes ashore.
July 10 Members of the expedition petition the Crown for recognition as a separate colony.
August 16 Cortés departs from Cempoala for the Mexican interior.
August–September War in Tlaxcala; alliance formed with Tlaxcalans.
October Castilians, Totonacs, and Tlaxcalans arrive in Cholula.
October 18 Advised by doña Marina of a trap, Cortés massacres the Cholulans.
November 8 Cortés enters the city of Mexico and meets Moctezuma.
Late November Uprising against Castilians on the coast; Moctezuma arrested as hostage.
December The instigator of the uprising, Cualpopoca, is burned at the stake in Mexico by the Castilians.

1520
Winter Cacama and Cuitláhuac plan uprising; Cacama arrested.
April Charles V receives the petition for

recognition of the Cortés expedition as a separate colonial venture.

April 20 An expeditionary force from Cuba under Pánfilo Narváez lands with orders to arrest Cortés and break up his expedition; Cortés leaves Mexico to confront Narváez, leaving Pedro de Alvarado in command.

May 16 Alvarado fires on the crowds during the Toxcatl celebration in the Temple Square.

May 27 Cortés defeats Narváez near Cempoala.

June 24 Cortés returns to Mexico. Castilians under siege.

June Moctezuma deposed. Cuitláhuac elected emperor. Moctezuma dies, probably of injuries received from stoning by angry crowds.

June 30 *Noche Triste*. Cortés leads his expedition out of Mexico. Caught on the causeway, many are slaughtered by the Mexicans.

Summer–autumn Smallpox epidemic breaks out. Cuitláhuac dies. Cuauhtémoc elected emperor.

June 30–July 10 Retreat from Mexico to Tlaxcala.

July 7 Battle of Otumba. Castilian cavalry saves expedition from complete annihilation.

August–September Cortés prepares for return to Mexico. Segura de la Frontera founded at Tepeac as a base.

December 26 Cortés begins advance toward Mexico from Segura.

1521

April 28 Thirteen brigantines launched on Lake Texcoco. City of Mexico put under blockade.

May 31 Gonzalo de Sandoval moves toward Iztapalapa, beginning the siege of Mexico.

May–August Siege continues.

August 13 Cuauhtémoc surrenders; Aztec empire ends.

1522

October 15 Charles V names Cortés governor and captain general of New Spain (Mexico).

1535

Conquistadors displaced by bureaucrats. Antonio de Mendoza becomes first viceroy of New Spain, inaugurating an administrative system that lasts until 1821.

Spain and Mexico in the 16th century

Spain

At the beginning of the 16th century Spain had only recently emerged from almost eight centuries of civil wars collectively called the *Reconquista* (Reconquest) or the Moorish Wars, when the northern kingdoms of the Iberian peninsula, Castile and Aragón, fought to recover the land conquered by the Moors in the 8th century. In 1492 Granada, the last bastion of Islamic rule, was recovered and in the same year Spain's Jewish population faced the choice between expulsion or conversion to Christianity. Although the *Reconquista* was regarded by Christian Spaniards as the expulsion of foreigners, the Moors had become such an integral part of Spanish society that they could no longer be called foreign. The same could be said of the nation's extensive Jewish population, which had made substantial contributions to philosophy, science, and economics.

During the final years of the Reconquest, the idea of Spain as a unified nation was a concept rather than a fact. The Iberian peninsula was essentially divided between three dominant kingdoms: Portugal to the west, Castile down the center, and Aragón to the east. Of the three, Portugal was the wealthiest and most powerful, but the least interested in Iberian affairs, being preoccupied with the developing African empire that was the source of its wealth and power. The others, Castile and Aragón, had managed to swallow most of the lesser kingdoms, leaving only two – Christian Navarre to the north, and Muslim Granada to the south – maintaining a precarious independence. A dynastic marriage between Queen Isabel of Castile and Crown Prince Ferdinand of Aragón in 1469 spelled the end of these two minor kingdoms and the conception, if not the birth, of a united Spain.

The first to fall was Granada, which surrendered in January 1492. This event, and the successful first voyage of Christopher Columbus of 1492–93, created a new sense of optimism, nationalism, and religious xenophobia. The Spaniards now saw themselves on a great national adventure tinged with religious evangelism. Patriotism and religious fervor were spurred ever onward by the promise of wealth. The first generation of voyagers – Columbus and his companions – were followed by an even more eager second generation. Between 1506 and 1518 some 200 ships made the passage from Spain to the Indies in search of new lands.

There were other, more tangible, motives. The leaders of expeditions of discovery and conquest often were members of the minor nobility, men with more pedigree than money or influence, who hoped to establish themselves both financially and politically by venturing to the Indies. The rank and file emigrated because farming in Castile had been replaced by the less labor-intensive stock raising. Many ordinary Castilians of the early 1500s faced poverty and hunger. Finally, there was the desire to be free, not only of the established hierarchy of Church and nobility, but of the growing new state bureaucracy as well.

For all the optimism and adventure, however, the discovery of what rapidly came to be called the New World was a traumatic event, not only for the Indians about to encounter European domination, but for the Europeans as well. Although the Renaissance brought an advance of culture and classical learning, the Europeans were totally unprepared for the discovery of new continents and their people. When their history, science, and philosophy could not explain the New World or its people, they turned to religion for answers to the unanswerable. It took centuries to truly understand what had happened, if, indeed, it is even yet understood. Faced with native peoples unlike any humans they had ever encountered, the Europeans were unsure whether they were of God or of the Devil. Did they have souls? Were they even human or merely a higher species of animal? The fact that the Indians themselves had, over thousands of years, developed a culture isolated from the rest of humanity and therefore alien to any conventional understanding, only aggravated the questions.

By 1517 Spaniards had established themselves not only in their initial foothold in Santo Domingo, but in Darien (Panama), Jamaica, and Cuba as well. Slaving expeditions had ventured into the islands of the Gulf of Honduras, and along the coasts of Nicaragua and Florida. The western Gulf of Mexico and northwestern Caribbean, however, were a void. To fill that void, the governor of Cuba, don Diego Velásquez, commissioned two expeditions, one under Francisco Hernández de Córdoba, in 1517,

A veteran of Columbus's second expedition in 1493, don Diego Velásquez (1464–1524) arrived in Cuba in 1511 to become the colony's first governor. Although he commissioned Cortés to explore the Mexican hinterland, he distrusted him, regarding him as a rival for the riches waiting to be exploited in the new colonies. (Museo Nacional de Antropologia, Mexico)

and a second under the governor's nephew, Juan de Grijalva, in 1518, to investigate the region.

Hernández de Córdoba and Grijalva explored the coasts of Yucatán and Campeche, formally taking possession on behalf of the Crown. Despite losses to Indian resistance, the two expeditions brought back reports of organized, well-populated cities, with a highly developed architecture. Governor Velásquez, who had applied to Spain for proconsulship of the newly discovered regions, decided a third expedition was in order, this one to be commanded by Hernán Cortés. Although Velásquez distrusted Cortés, and the latter's military experience was limited to the relatively simple conquest of Cuba, he was nevertheless a powerfully wealthy force in Cuban politics, and a shrewd judge of men. He had money and credit to risk, while the governor was loathe to risk his own. It is doubtful anyone envisioned that his appointment would change the history of the world – except, perhaps, Cortés himself.

This remarkable man was born in Medellín in 1485, the son of don Martín Cortés de Monroy, and his wife, doña Catalina Pizarro de Altamirano, both members of minor nobility. As a youth, he was sickly, and nearly died several times. In the religiously charged atmosphere of the era, his survival was attributed to St. Peter, whom he invoked on any great undertaking in later life. At 14 he was sent to the university at Salamanca, where he studied law, and, although capable, was bored and indifferent. After two years he used lack of funds and chronic illness as an excuse to drop out and return home. After that he wandered aimlessly about Spain for a year, no doubt hearing stories of the Indies from sailors and adventurers in the country's southern ports. In 1504 he set sail for Santo Domingo, where he obtained a grant of land and Indians. Through a family friendship with the governor, don Nicolás de Ovando, Cortés also was appointed notary of the town council of Azúa, a position with actual legal power when compared to its English or American counterparts.

Hernán Cortés (1485–1547). Ruthless, single-minded and ambitious, Cortés's determination and bravery established the Spanish hegemony in the New World, and destroyed the Aztec civilization. His intelligence and ability to work with the Indians meant his expedition succeeded where others had failed. (Ann Ronan Picture Library)

By 1511 Cortés was a successful planter in Santo Domingo. Nevertheless, he accompanied Velásquez in the conquest of Cuba, serving as clerk to the treasurer. He received a grant of Indians which he shared with Juan Juárez, whose sister, Catalina, he married. Cortés's position soon brought him into conflict with Velásquez. Both were strong willed, and each was determined to be the dominant force in Cuban affairs. Cortés headed a faction that quietly worked to undermine Velásquez, and the shrewd governor was fully aware of it. Neither, however, was strong enough to subvert the other, and an uneasy alliance ensued, occasionally punctuated by open feuding. This was one of the considerations that prompted Velásquez to place Cortés in charge of the expedition to Mexico; he had a competent man in charge, while at the same time rid himself of a nuisance. He little realized that he was letting the jinni out of the bottle.

Mexico

The Aztecs, or Mexicans as they preferred to be called, were the latest and mightiest of a chain of civilizations that had dominated the central plateau of Mexico for over 1,500 years. They were not an empire in the modern sense of a central imperial authority which, through its own officials, holds direct suzerainty over its dominions; rather, there was a tributary overlordship vested in the city of Mexico. The adjacent city-states were bound to Mexico by treaty. Beyond were numerous vassal states, internally self-governing, but forced by a highly developed policy of terror to acknowledge Mexico's supremacy, pay it tribute, and submit to its demands.

The Aztecs were not indigenous to central Mexico, having arrived only a few centuries earlier from some vague and remote region to the northwest. Their origins are shrouded in myth, confused even more by the fact that as they grew from obscurity to dominance, they reinvented their history to suit their rising status. They appear to have been the last of several waves of alien peoples of the Nahua language group, who entered the region in the centuries following the decline of the great city-state of Teotihuacán, the ruins of which are some 30 miles northeast of Mexico City. According to their own early accounts, they came from a place called Aztlán, hence the name "Aztec" (people of Aztlán). Aztlán was the site of the Seven Caves of Chicomoztoc, from which the Nahua people emerged in seven separate

waves, among which were the Culhua, or Toltecs, whose civilization Mexico adopted and supplanted, and the Tlaxcalans, who later became Hernán Cortés's most valuable allies. Fra Diego Durán, a Dominican who compiled their history in the 16th century, believed the emergence, which is to say the migrations, began about AD 820. It continued over a period of many years, until, by 1064, the Aztecs themselves, the last and most beloved of the gods (according to their legends), emerged.

Over the ensuing centuries, the Aztecs wandered throughout much of western Mexico, driven by a prophecy from their god, Huitzilopochtli, that they were a chosen people, and he would lead them to a promised land. In every new region they established settlements, usually having to fight the indigenous peoples. Always, their god uprooted them and drove them onward. About 1168, they arrived at Tula, capital of the now declining Toltec Empire, where they seem to have settled for a while, and began acquiring a veneer of the local culture. Nevertheless, they again uprooted themselves, forced onward by the ancient prophecy.

By 1299 the Aztecs appear to have reached the Valley of Mexico with its four vast, interconnected lakes, Xaltocán (or Zumpango) in the north, Texcoco, the largest, in the center, Xochimilco to the south, and Chalco to the southeast. The lakes were surrounded by city-states which were the remnants of the old Toltec domains. Here, on a mud-flat in the middle of Lake Texcoco, the Aztecs saw a vision of an eagle resting on a *tenochca* or nopal cactus, fulfilling the prophecy of their promised land. This pivotal event, traditionally dated at 1325, marks the founding of the city of Mexico, then known as Tenochtitlán.

By the late 14th century, the city maintained a precarious independence as a vassal to the more powerful Tepanecs, whose seat was the city of Tlacopán. Slowly, however, the Aztecs worked to build both their population and their prestige. In a region where pedigree determined status, they began to create a heritage for themselves, much as the Romans in similar circumstances recast themselves as descendants of the Trojans of Aeneas. In 1376 they chose as their ruler Acampichtli, the son of an Aztec warrior and a princess from the city of Culhuacán. Through his grandfather, the Culhua king Nauhyotl, Acampichtli could claim decent from the ancient Toltec rulers, and he strengthened the claim by marrying some 20 princesses of surrounding cities, all descendants of Toltec royalty. Although Acampichtli remained a vassal of the Tepanecs, he nevertheless founded the royal line that ended with the Conquest in 1521.

In 1428 Acampichtli's son, Itzcoatl, ascended to power. (He was the fourth king of Tenochtitlán and succeeded his half-brother Huitzihuitl.) One of his first acts was to form an alliance with Nezahualcoyotl, head of the extraordinarily gifted dynasty that ruled the city of Texcoco. (The dynasty that ruled Texcoco was ancient, known for the wisdom of its rulers, who were gifted diplomats, philosophers, and poets, all of whom were very highly regarded.) Together, they waged a victorious war against Tlacopán, gaining complete independence for Tenochtitlán. Rather than subjugating the Tepanecs, however, they invited them to join their entente, inaugurating what became known at the Triple Alliance, which dominated affairs in central Mexico for almost a century thereafter. Each of the three city-states remained independent, with Tenochtitlán ruling over the area populated by the Aztecs, Texcoco over the Aculhua-Chichimecs, and Tlacopán (later known as Tacuba) over the Tepanecs. Together, they extended their realm beyond the valley, dividing the conquered towns and cities equally but with all tribute paid to the Triple Alliance as a whole. In this way, the Aztecs of Tenochtitlán rose to dominance, with Texcoco and Tlacopán existing as semi-client states.

The Triple Alliance marked the birth of the Aztec Empire, and Itzcoatl became the first *huey tlatoani*, a title literally meaning "great spokesman [for the empire];" Europeans translated it as "emperor." Eager to legitimize his position and that of his city, he ordered the destruction of old codices that recorded the Aztecs' nomadic past. Where Toltec legends held that the earth's existence had been marked by four great ages or "suns," the Aztecs added a fifth – their own. Even the term "Aztec," a reminder of their humble origins in Aztlán, was suppressed. Henceforth, they were the Culhua-Mexica, or Mexicans. Nevertheless, to the very end, they were self-conscious of the fact that they were foreigners. In the recesses of their minds, they believed that just as they had conquered and subjugated the natives, so others might conquer and subjugate them.

Over the ensuing decades, the might of the empire grew. Aside from the conquest of tributary states, a trading network covered much of Middle America. The city of Mexico, as Tenochtitlán was now called, became wealthy and powerful, and the successive emperors – Moctezuma I, Axayácatl, Tizoc, and Ahuítzotl – were as renowned in their world as the Caesars were in theirs.

With the accession of Moctezuma II in about 1503, the empire reached its height. A competent general, Moctezuma put down rebellions in the provinces, and conquered new ones. The only parts of the country that were able to resist Mexican rule were the powerful Tarascan empire of the west, in modern Jalisco and Michoacán, and the small, militant republic of Tlaxcala in the

The founding and expansion of the city of Tenochtitlán, Mexico from the *Codex Mendoza*. The eagle on the cactus represents the founding of the city, while the shield over a bundle of arrows (symbolizing war), decorated with seven balls (representing power), represents the city itself. Immediately in front of the eagle is the symbol of a *tzompantli* or skull rack. The figures surrounding it are the tribal leaders who founded the city. The symbols on the bottom represent the Aztec conquest of the adjacent cities of Culhuacan (left) and Tenayuca (right), which subsequently became tributary vassals. The whole is framed in the names of the years of the Aztec calendar, such as 13 reed, 12 rabbit, 11 house, 10 knife, etc., to chronicle the first calendar cycle of the city's existence. (Bodleian Library, Oxford)

east. The Mexicans tended to leave the Tarascans alone, because the Tarascan Empire, while less developed, was powerful enough to fight it to a standstill and inflict severe damage. However, a state of cold war existed with Tlaxcala and its allies, and frequently it broke into open fighting. When enemy prisoners were captured, they were offered up as sacrifices to the Mexican gods. The same happened to Mexican soldiers who were taken by their enemies. In either case, the victims were considered beloved of the gods, and, it was believed, would go directly to paradise. After one defeat, Moctezuma was informed of the sacrifice of Mexican prisoners by the victorious people of Huexotzingo. "For this fate we have been born," he observed, "for this we go into battle, and death in this manner is fortunate. That is the blessed death that our ancestors extolled."

The *tzompantli* altar at the *Templo Mayor* (Great Temple) in Mexico. (Topham Picturepoint)

RIGHT The elaborate costumes of Mexican warriors were designed as much to intimidate their opponents as to protect the combatants themselves. (*Codex Mendoza*, Folio 67r; Bodleian Library, Oxford)

Mexican religious beliefs

Human sacrifice was paramount in Mexican religion, and the Mexicans took it to the extreme. Countless people – slaves, captives, human levies of tribute from the provinces, children of the poor – died on the temples each year. Their blood was shed to postpone the inevitable death of the fifth sun, the sun of the Mexicans. They believed it would be the last sun, and when it died, the world would rise no more. Gods had given their own blood

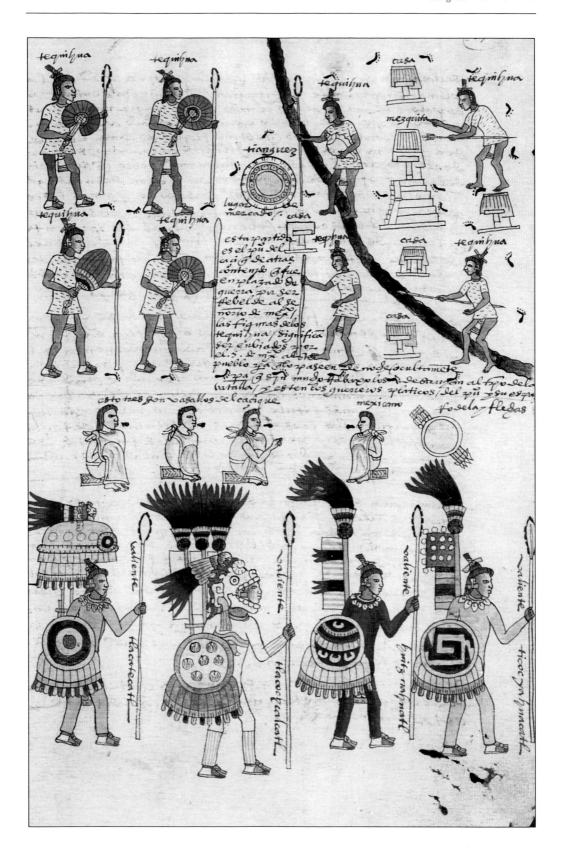

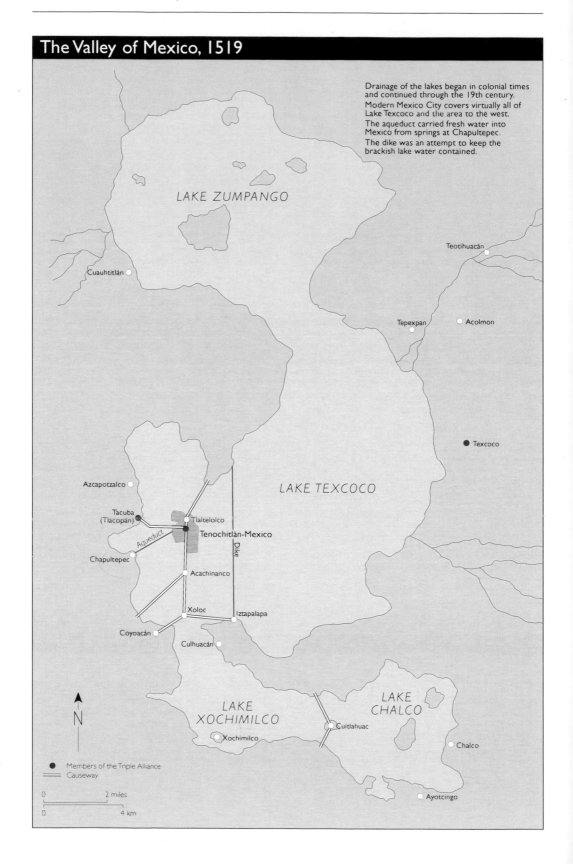

The Valley of Mexico, 1519

Drainage of the lakes began in colonial times and continued through the 19th century.

Modern Mexico City covers virtually all of Lake Texcoco and the area to the west.

The aqueduct carried fresh water into Mexico from springs at Chapultepec.

The dike was an attempt to keep the brackish lake water contained.

LAKE ZUMPANGO

Teotihuacán

Cuauhtitlán

Tepexpan   Acolmon

Azcapotzalco

Texcoco

LAKE TEXCOCO

Tacuba
(Tlacopán)   Tlatelolco

Tenochtitlán-Mexico

Chapultepec

Aqueduct

Dike

Acachinanco

Xoloc

Iztapalapa

Coyoacán

Culhuacán

LAKE
XOCHIMILCO

LAKE
CHALCO

N

Cuitlahuac

Xochimilco

Chalco

● Members of the Triple Alliance
═══ Causeway

Ayotcingo

0   2 miles

0   4 km

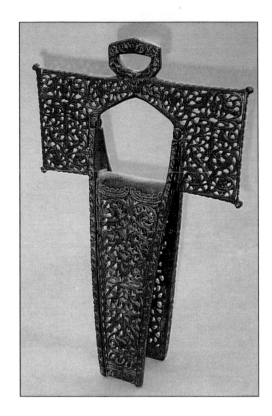

A Castilian stirrup of the Conquest period, cast from heavy iron filigree in the form of a cross. As much weapon as horse furniture, it could be slammed into the head of a foot soldier in close combat. (Enrique E. Guerra Collection)

to create this sun, and without blood, it would die. The blood of the gods themselves had to be replenished, or they, too, would die. In short, their religion offered no hope, only doom. Despite their outward ostentation and arrogance, subconsciously the Mexicans prepared for the worst.

Toward the end of the first decade of the 16th century, the appearance of a comet set off a chain of omens that appeared over the ensuing years and foretold the end of the empire. The comet was followed by a fire that destroyed the Temple of Huitzilopochtli, and the destruction of a second temple by a bolt of lightning, both signs of defeat and conquest. On a calm, still day, the waters of Lake Texcoco rose and flooded the city, destroying many houses. Then, a phantom woman appeared in the night, wailing, "O my beloved sons, now we are at the point of going! My beloved sons, whither shall I take you?" (This particular phantom has passed into modern Mexican folklore as "the llorona," the weeping woman, who is used to frighten children.) Other omens and visions appeared, including one of armed men riding on large animals that appeared to be deer.

Some of these events have rational explanations and were simply natural phenomena: comets appear, lightning strikes, and buildings burn. Geologically, Mexico is extremely unstable, and a distant earthquake easily could have caused the lake to overflow. Yet for all their architecture, organizational ability, and military skill, the Mexicans (like their European counterparts) simply did not understand the natural forces

that affected them. Thus, it was easy for their imaginations to make the jump from reality to fantasy, just as it was easy for the New England Puritans, more than a century later, to regard natural occurrences as signs of God's pleasure or wrath.

As high priest of a fatalistic religion, Moctezuma could only surmise that the sun of the Aztecs was nearing its end. In 1519, when couriers from the east coast brought word of newcomers mounted on strange beasts, he appears to have expected it. He was aware of the Castilian presence in the Gulf of Mexico and Central America; the Mexican trade network was extensive, and so was its intelligence capabilities. In fact, the arrival of Europeans in the region had already worked its way into the latest round of religion and prophecy.

A war between gods

The Spanish soldier

In his pioneering *History of Mexico*, Hubert Howe Bancroft described the 16th-century conquistador as being "of different material from the soldier of the present day." Apparently, "He was not a mere machine; he was a great dealer in destiny. He would willingly adventure his life. If he lost, it was well; if he won, it was better. A hundred did lose where one gained, and this each might have known to be the risk had he taken the trouble to make a computation. His life was but one continuous game of hazard; but, if successful, he expected wealth and glory as a just reward."

In short, he was not a soldier in the conventional sense. Although many of those who accompanied Cortés did have formal military backgrounds in the Italian campaigns and elsewhere, they were essentially a company of adventurers. They paid their own way, often contributing to the overall cost of the expedition, and many had to take out loans in order to meet their expenses. Even Cortés himself borrowed heavily from the merchants of Cuba, offering his estates and Indian chattels as security. Their reward, if any, would be shares in the spoils of what they hoped would be a successful and lucrative expedition.

War and adventure were in their blood. A large percentage was not simply from Spain, but from Castile, the country that for centuries had been at the forefront of the wars against the Moors. Narrowing it down even further, the two greatest conquerors, Cortés of Mexico and his very distant cousin, Francisco Pizarro of Peru, were from the Castilian province of Extremadura. Literally translated as "Hard Extreme," Extremadura was also the extremity on the frontier between Christian Spain and Muslim Spain,

and the battleground where the two forces so often clashed. A high, bleak plateau of windswept plains, large tracts of tough, gnarled oaks, and an overabundance of fortresses, it has always bred a hard, lonely, self-reliant people.

The terrain was only part of the force that forged the regional character. There was also a culture of war, a centuries-old crusading spirit against the infidel, a feeling of righteousness in the cause of Christianity. The end of the Moorish Wars in 1492 removed one infidel threat from the scene, but the void would be filled as the voyages of Christopher Columbus and his successors provided new ones. Extremadura was more than ready to provide the great captains of the Conquest, who then enlisted fellow Extremadurans to form the core of the invasion forces.

The backbone of this army was the ordinary infantryman, who was invariably a swordsman. Additionally, Bernal Díaz, the conquistador whose memoirs provide the most detailed account of the Cortés expedition, listed various specialists, including 15 horsemen, as well as crossbowmen and musketeers. These men incurred further expenses in weaponry and mounts. Besides their food and equipment, all soldiers paid what they considered exorbitant fees to the expedition surgeons who treated their wounds and tropical fevers, and to the apothecaries who provided the medicines.

The cannon was the first practical firearm, and six were carried on the Cortés expedition. One, a crude Lombard, is on display in the Conquest Hall at the National Museum of History in Chapultepec Castle in Mexico City. Smaller weapons evolved from the cannon until, by the mid-15th century, a practical shoulder arm had been developed in the form

ABOVE The casque helmet, which was hammered and riveted together, was much simpler and less ornate than the morion, and would have been used by the ordinary soldier who had the means to buy it. (Enrique E. Guerra Collection)

RIGHT This Castilian broadsword, discovered recently in Mexico City, may well be an actual relic of the Conquest. It was recovered from the site of an ancient canal on Cortés's line of retreat during the *Noche Triste*. (Enrique E. Guerra Collection)

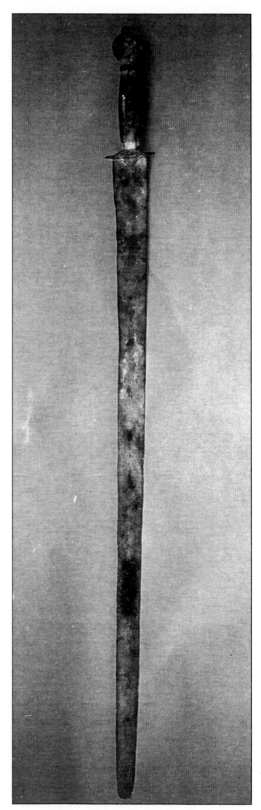

of the matchlock musket, such as that carried by the harquebusiers or musketeers of the Conquest. The matchlock was a heavy-caliber muzzle-loading weapon, with a long barrel fastened to a shoulder stock. The firing mechanism consisted of a long cotton cord or "match" soaked in a saltpeter solution and allowed to dry. It was inserted into a hammer-like mechanism and set alight, providing a slow burn. When the trigger was pulled, the mechanism brought the glowing tip of the match down onto a priming charge that ignited the powder inside the barrel. These weapons were heavy and clumsy, and

BELOW The morion helmet and upper body armor were expensive in the early 16th century, and would have been worn by officers and other men of means on the expedition. The ordinary soldier generally was less well protected, and often adopted the indigenous quilted armor. (Enrique E. Guerra Collection)

quilted cotton armor of the Aztecs, which was light, allowed freedom of movement, and provided reasonable protection against the darts and sling stones of the natives. The soldiers also carried shields, often of wood covered by rawhide.

The Mexican soldier

The Mexican army, whether Aztec proper or from one of the surrounding principalities, was one of the very few instances in the New World where Europeans encountered members of a formal, organized military establishment, rather than tribal warriors. A Spaniard known to history only as the "Anonymous Conquistador," wrote: "It is one of the most beautiful sights in the world to see them in their battle array because they keep formation wonderfully and are very handsome. . . Anyone facing them for the first time can be terrified by their screams and their ferocity. In warfare they are the most cruel people to be found, for they spare neither brothers, relatives, friends, nor women even if they are beautiful; they kill them all and eat them. When they cannot take the enemy plunder and booty with them, they burn everything."

By killing and eating, the conquistador undoubtedly meant capturing victims for sacrifice. Taking captives for sacrifice was the great testimony to the warrior's prowess in battle. The novice soldier's designation as a captor, particularly if he acted alone, was an occasion of great ceremony. As the number of his captives rose, so did his prestige, until he, too, became a seasoned warrior and a master of trainees in the schools.

Depending on family background and social status, boys were sent to one of two schools, the *telpochcalli* for commoners, or the *calmecac* for the children of nobles. These schools offered training in a variety of fields, including the military. The sons of nobles and soldiers were most likely to take up the

the musketeer had to support the forward part of the gun on a shooting stick. A sudden gust of wind, or drizzling rain extinguished the match, rendering the weapon useless under many conditions. Thus, despite the development of firearms, the archer or crossbowman continued to be essential for fighting at a distance.

The captains and cavalry wore steel armor. The men, few of whom could afford European armor, very early adopted the

RIGHT Examples of tribute paid to Mexico by its vassals. (Codex Mendoza, Folio 20r; Bodleian Library, Oxford)

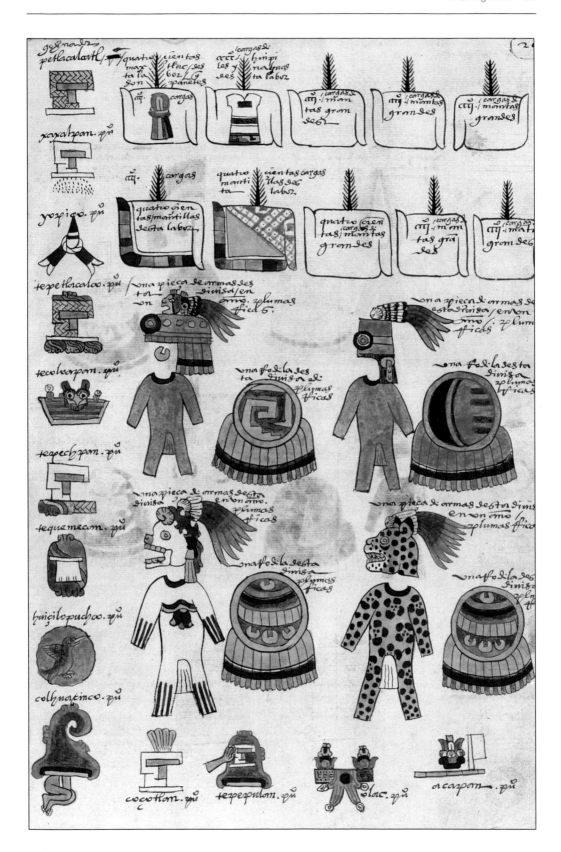

As heavy armor began to prove unsuitable for the terrain and methods of combat in Mexico, conquistadors sometimes carved a piece from their cuirasses, covered the sharp edges with rawhide, and wore them over the chest area. Much lighter than the full breastplate, it allowed the soldier more freedom of movement, but was heavy enough to ward off most native weapons. This example is decorated with a cross. (Enrique E. Guerra Collection)

warrior's profession themselves. They were turned over to war captains, training officers, and veteran warriors, who trained the boys in archery, dart throwing from an *atlatl* (a throwing stick that gave extra leverage to a spear or dart), swordsmanship, and use of the shield in combat. When the veterans went to war, they often took boy trainees along to handle their weapons, much as the knights of medieval Europe employed a squire.

Although there was a hierarchy with a ranking system comparable to a modern army, the Aztec soldier was not a member of a large, monolithic force as is understood today. His loyalty was severally and variously tied to his ward or district in the city, the headman of that ward, the emperor, the state, and other interests. In this sense, he might be compared to the volunteer soldier of the Union Army during the American Civil War, who had divided loyalties to entities such as his county, state, and to the federal government.

Considering that they were essentially a primitive people, Mexican warriors were well armed for combat by the standards of the 16th century. Although they did not have metal weapons or firearms, they were experts in bow and arrow, lance, blowgun, dart, and sling. They also carried a *tepoztopilli*, a thrusting spear similar to that used by the Zulus in the 19th century. But whereas the

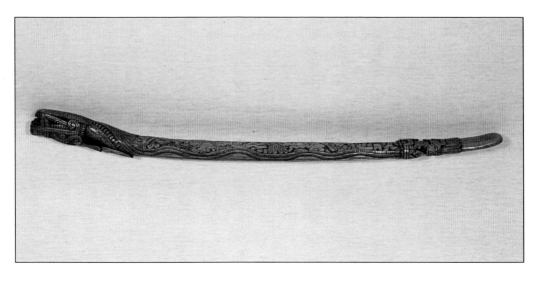

Aztec *atlatl* or dart thrower. (Museo Nacional de Antropologia, Mexico)

Zulu blade was steel, the Mexican blade was wood, edged with razor-sharp pieces of obsidian, and could slash as well as thrust. The grip also was substantially longer. Slings were among the most effective weapons, and the Castilians regarded them with a healthy respect. A large shower of stones unleashed and smashing into an enemy simultaneously caused substantial casualties, and even heavily armored Europeans suffered serious injuries. One of the most vicious weapons was the *macauhuitl*, a one-piece wooden sword with a blade edged on both sides by obsidian. These came in one- or two-handed versions, and when wielded by well-trained warriors were deadly.

Mexican armor was of quilted cotton, and was so thick it could resist an arrow or a dart. For that reason, the Castilians also found it practical. The Mexicans wore it under a war suit which, though not quilted, afforded some overall protection to the body. Suits were decorated, with fine featherwork being reserved for the ranking warriors. Nobles wore war suits of animal skins.

Helmets took the form of eagles, jaguars, or other symbols that could designate rank or military order. Often they were made of wood and bone, heavily decorated with featherwork. When a military order had a large totemic animal, like a jaguar, wolf, or puma, the actual head of the animal might be mounted over a frame of wood or a quilted cotton liner, with the warrior looking through the animal's mouth. Besides being defensive, these war suits and helmets were designed for psychological impact, to terrify an enemy. Warriors carried shields of hide or woven plant fibers, often backed by quilting. Ceremonial shields, such as those sent to Europe by Cortés, were highly decorated with gold, precious stones, and featherwork. Even the war shields, however, had a feathered fringe hanging down from the bottom that could deflect an arrow or dart and protect the legs. Surviving examples may be seen in Vienna, Stuttgart, and Chapultepec Castle in Mexico City.

As well as wars of conquest and subjugation, the Mexicans engaged in events known as "flower wars." These wars were fought by prearrangement with a selected enemy for the sole purpose of providing the blood of captive warriors for the altars on the temples in the Mexican capital. Besides bringing in new sacrificial victims, it also

OVERLEAF A view of the Plumed Serpent Temple at Teotihuacan with the carved heads of the Quetzalcoatl, the Plumed Serpent god, and Tlaloc, the goggle-eyed god of rain. This building was built centuries before the arrival of the Aztecs, who adopted these and many other native gods into their own pantheon. (©Philip Baird www.anthroarcheart.org)

Shield decorated with a panel of feather mosaic forming the name-glyph of King Ahuitzotl. Probably obtained by Cortés from Moctezuma. (Ann Ronan Picture Library).

gave practical combat experience to young warriors newly emerged from training. Companies were organized to assure a suitable mixing of new recruits with seasoned veterans. The arrangements made, the armies of Mexico and its allies would march on the enemy. Every effort would be made to avoid killing enemy warriors in order that they could be captured and returned to Mexico as offerings to the gods.

Fra Durán described one scene in 1487, in which 80,400 captives were sacrificed at the dedication of the Great Temple, the victims lined up on the causeways according to which allied army captured them.

Thus, as the Aztec Empire's power expanded over more of the region, war became less of a practical art and more of a ritual used to gain tribute and feed the gods. Meanwhile, hatred smoldered in the tributary states, which provided not only treasure for the empire but victims for its sacrifices, and in 1519 Cortés had remarkably little trouble recruiting them as allies and auxiliaries. When confronted by a grim, determined enemy, fighting a European war by European tactics and for European goals, and when that enemy was supported by hordes of local auxiliaries, the Aztec military mentality was unable to adjust. Even in the final desperate days of their national existence, they took captives rather than trying to destroy their enemies on the spot.

The Conquest was not simply a war between soldiers, but a confrontation between civilizations and especially between gods. The Aztecs' own fatalism and obsession with ritual played a major part in their downfall. They knew that their gods were demanding and capricious, who could give or withhold their beneficence on a whim. They believed that the world had been destroyed four times before. It would be destroyed again. The Aztecs themselves were foreigners who had displaced the native peoples of the valley and beyond, and they, too, would be displaced. There had been prophecies of doom, and there had been omens. Now, it seemed as though all the elements of their destruction were falling into place. Yet they would hold out and fight until the end, because they were warriors who accepted the decisions of their gods without question.

On the Spanish side, Cortés's men fought with grim desperation, when the object was no longer riches, nor even their lives, but the fate of their souls. They knew full well that if captured, they would be dragged to the tops of the temples and offered up as sacrifices to idols that they literally believed were manifestations of Satan and his demons. They had seen these monstrous idols covered in blood, described as demons by Old Testament prophets in the Revelation of St. John and by a thousand years of Christianity. Yet they also knew, through the teachings of Christ, that in the end they must triumph. In their own lifetimes they had witnessed the end of eight centuries of Islam in Spain. And in overthrowing the idols and conquering the idolaters they believed they were carrying Christ's mandate to take His word to all the world. If they died, sword in hand, fighting against these demon gods, their salvation was assured.

Divide and conquer

The arrangement between Diego Velásquez and Hernán Cortés called for the governor to provide two or three ships, with Cortés funding the balance of the expedition. Cortés moved rapidly, assembling his own group of captains, including Pedro de Alvarado, who would serve more or less as his right hand throughout the Conquest. Alvarado was ruthless and rash, often prone to acting without considering the consequences; but he was a man who would be loyal to Cortés until the end. Others, likewise, could be counted on to support Cortés in any showdown, among them Cristóbal de Olíd and Gonzalo Sandoval. As for the men, the lure of shares in any profit was enough to draw ample recruits from the rootless young adventurers in Cuba, among them a Castilian of good family and little means named Bernal Díaz del Castillo, whose later account would become one of the greatest sources of information on the Conquest.

Watching the preparations in Santiago de Cuba, Velásquez became alarmed at their speed and thoroughness, and feared (with good reason as it turned out) that Cortés might have his own agenda. For his part, Cortés began to suspect that the governor would grab the wealth and glory of a successful expedition, and redoubled his efforts to retain control. Finally, Velásquez forced the issue, and sent orders removing Cortés from command and detaining the expedition. But Cortés had second-guessed him and, on November 18, 1518, ordered the expedition to sail from Santiago, putting in first at Trinidad and, later, San Cristóbal de la Habana to complete fitting out. (On the southern coast of Cuba; modern Havana was known as Puerto de Carenas.) Altogether, the fleet that left San Cristóbal on February 10, 1519 consisted of 11 vessels, four of them decked ships, and the rest open brigantines. There were 530 Europeans, several hundred West Indian natives and Africans, as well as about eight European women. Livestock included 16 horses, an animal never before seen on the American mainland, and a large number of war dogs, large wolfhounds and mastiffs, used in Europe to attack the enemy and tear him apart.

Arms included crossbows, harquebuses, and artillery, as well as flags. Cortés's own standard was blue and white with a red cross in the center. Emblazoned on it was a motto reminiscent of Constantine the Great, *Amici, sequamor crucem, et si nos fidem habemus, vere in hoc signo vicemus* ("Friends, let us follow the cross, and if we have faith, truly by this sign we shall conquer"). Cortés dedicated the expedition itself to St. Peter, who he believed took a special interest in his safety.

The initial landing

In the Yucatán Channel heavy weather scattered the fleet and, according to a prearranged plan, the ships rendezvoused at Cozumel, off the west coast of the Yucatán Peninsula, an island already well known to Spanish pilots. About one-third of his men had already been there with Grijalva. Here, Cortés was at his best, treating the locals in such a friendly manner that he had little trouble establishing contact. Communication was through the broken Castilian of "Old Melchor," a Maya who had been taken to Cuba on the Córdoba expedition of 1517. Soon, however, they received an unexpected bonus in the person of Jerónimo de Aguilar, an Andalusian cleric who had been shipwrecked on the island in 1511, and who now spoke fluent Chontol Maya. One of two survivors of the wreck, he readily joined the expedition. His companion, Gonzalo Guerrero, however, had married into the local nobility with a high position, and ignored letters inviting him to be repatriated.

The stay in Cozumel gave Cortés time to plan his next move, and to accustom his band of mercenaries and adventurers to working together as a cohesive, disciplined unit. Sailing from Cozumel, the fleet touched at nearby Isla Mujeres, then continued on around the Yucatán Peninsula to Tabasco, in the Gulf of Mexico. On March 22 they entered the waterway now known as the Rio Grijalva, where Cortés, through Aguilar, attempted a parley with natives from the nearby town of Potonchán. The locals, however, were hostile and, the following day, he forced his way ashore. The decisive fight came on Annunciation Day, March 25. Whipped up by Old Melchor, who had escaped and joined them, the Indians fought fiercely, but the landing of the horses, and the new experience of a cavalry charge sent them fleeing in panic.

The large numbers of native warriors and their tough resistance convinced Cortés that force would not be enough to subjugate the mainland peoples, as it had been with the islands of the Indies. The key would be diplomacy, to overawe with words, and with display, and to look for and exploit weaknesses and factionalism.

Summoning the chiefs, he told them that if they became vassals of the Spanish Crown, as were the Castilians themselves, he would protect them. Otherwise, he said the artillery (which he represented as living creatures), would jump up and kill them. That was the signal for one of the gunners to fire his piece. At the same moment, one of the more assertive stallions was allowed to scent a mare that had recently foaled, and he began to paw and buck. The terrified chiefs immediately submitted and the following morning brought gifts of gold, fine cloth, along with 20 women to serve the Castilians as "wives." Asked where the gold originated, they answered "Culhua," referring to the

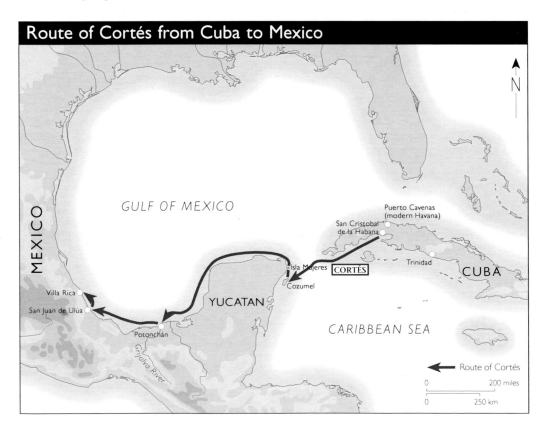

Route of Cortés from Cuba to Mexico

GULF OF MEXICO

MEXICO

Puerto Cavenas (modern Havana)

San Cristobal de la Habana

Trinidad

Isla Mujeres   CORTÉS

Cozumel

CUBA

Villa Rica

YUCATAN

San Juan de Ulúa

CARIBBEAN SEA

Potonchán

Grijalva River

⟵ Route of Cortés

0   200 miles

0   250 km

Valley of Mexico, and "Mexico," referring to the Aztec capital itself.

Cortés and his men now determined to visit Mexico to see for themselves the source of this wealth. The most important gift from the chiefs of Potonchán suddenly became one of the women, a girl in her late teens named Malinalli. Renamed doña Marina, she spoke both Nahuatl and Chontol, so she could communicate with the Mexicans and with Aguilar, and thus became Cortés's ears and mouthpiece. Years later in his account of the Conquest, Bernal Díaz would write, "Doña Marina in all the wars of New Spain and Tlaxcala and Mexico was a most excellent woman and good interpreter . . . [and] in this capacity she always accompanied Cortés." Almost as an afterthought, he added she also became Cortés's mistress and bore him a son.

Getting under way again, the fleet sailed for four days, arriving at the island of San Juan de Ulúa, at the entrance to the modern harbor of Veracruz, on Maundy Thursday. Although this was the country of the Totonacs, a people subject to Mexico, the dignitaries who came out in canoes appear to have been Mexican. Inviting them on board his ship for dinner, Cortés told them through Aguilar and doña Marina that he came as a friend to trade and explore. The following day, he led his men ashore, setting up camp with an altar to celebrate Good Friday Mass. All the while, more dignitaries were arriving, culminating on Easter Sunday with a visit from Teuhtlilli, a sort of governor apparently charged with overseeing Mexican affairs in the province and keeping the Totonacs in line.

Cortés explained his mission, and said he looked forward to meeting Moctezuma. Teuhtlilli replied that this was impossible. However, the emperor had sent magnificent gifts of gold, cloth, and featherwork. Cortés responded by giving European goods unfamiliar in the New World, such as glass beads and a finely carved chair. His men demonstrated their horsemanship skills and mastery of artillery before the governor.

Teuhtlilli departed, returning again in a few days with even greater treasures, among them a gigantic, beautifully decorated golden disc representing the sun, and a slightly smaller one representing the moon. Before leaving, he had borrowed a European helmet, and now returned it filled to the top with gold dust. A meeting between Cortés and the emperor, however, was apparently impossible.

Moctezuma's reasons for offering these great treasures have been debated for almost five centuries. Was he trying to bribe the Castilians into leaving? Or was he attempting, as often was done in the Orient, to overawe these foreigners with his wealth and power? Whatever the motive, it only excited the Castilians, and made them more determined to visit the source of such wealth. The problem was that the camp was divided into two factions: the supporters of Diego Velásquez, who wanted to take what had been gained so far and depart for Cuba, and the rank and file, who saw little advantage in supporting the governor but unlimited opportunities in moving ahead.

Cortés's position was simple. He had to conquer or die. If he returned to Cuba, he faced imprisonment or death for sailing in defiance of the governor. To advance on his own would make him a traitor to the Crown – unless he were backed by a legally constituted authority. His brief training in law had prepared him for this day. He resigned the commission given him by Velásquez, thus absolving him of all allegiance to the governor, persuaded the men to form a municipal government, designated Villa Rica de la Vera Cruz ("Rich Town of the True Cross"[1]), and petitioned the king to recognize it as a colony, with Cortés as captain and chief justice. The treasure accumulated to date was inventoried and loaded aboard ship to accompany Cortés's representatives, Alonso Hernández Puertocarrero and Francisco de Montejo, back to Spain. This, technically, was a pledge of good faith, but in fact was a bribe to the avaricious King Charles.

---

1 Villa Rica was subsequently moved 40 miles north up the coast, where the Castilians established the first permanent town, now a ruin.

The landing of the Castilians, from the *Florentine Codex*, Plate 1. (American Museum of Natural History)

While camped on the coast, the Castilians were visited by a delegation from the principal Totonac city of Cempoala, whose primary mission seemed to have been to assess the potential of these strangers as allies against their Mexican overlords. Taking the bulk of his force, Cortés marched inland to the city, which had been wealthy and powerful in its own right, although was now a tributary to Mexico. Here, the Castilians saw the first examples of the magnificent architecture and large populations they would increasingly encounter as they moved inland. They also saw very real indications of extensive human sacrifice on the blood-soaked temples.

The Totonacs apparently were on the verge of rebellion, and Cortés played this to his advantage. By lucky coincidence, the Mexican tribute gatherers arrived in the Totonac towns. Angry that the Castilians had been received without permission, they demanded, in addition to the usual tribute, 20 men and women for sacrifice. Cortés convinced the Totonacs to arrest them, saying the Spanish Crown intended to end such abuses. The proud officials were dragged through the streets in halters, and one was flogged. That night, however, they were permitted to escape, and returned to Mexico with the news of a rebellion. Then, in an even more daring move, Cortés ordered the idols thrown down from the Totonac temples, smashed to pieces and burned. When the people tried to stop it, their chiefs and priests were surrounded, and Cortés said they would be killed on the first show of hostility. Having defied their overlords, and with their religion destroyed, the Totonacs were now committed to the Castilian cause beyond any possibility of turning back.

There remained one last piece of unfinished business: a growing rebellion in the Velásquez faction, whose members planned to seize one of the ships and return to Cuba. Moving swiftly, Cortés hanged one of their leaders. Then, having removed

The square at Cempoala was the scene of pivotal events of the Conquest, including the first alliance with native states, the first overthrow of the native idols, and Cortés's defeat of a rival expedition sent from Cuba under Panfilo de Narváez. (Instituto Nacional de Antropologia e Historia, Mexico)

everything of any possible use, he scuttled his fleet. Like their leader, the men were now faced with two options: conquer or die.

On August 16, Cortés left Cempoala for the interior. Passing through the town of Zautla, he heard, for the first time, a detailed description of the city of Mexico, which filled the men with both excitement and fear. Continuing on up through the Valley of Zautla, they reached a wall built across the western mouth which, they were told, marked the territory of Tlaxcala, a loose confederation of four cities centered around the city of Tlaxcala itself. Locals advised him to stay clear of the country, because the Tlaxcalans were mortal enemies of the Mexicans; if they knew the Castilians were going to Mexico, they would attack. The Totonacs, however, advised continuing because Tlaxcala would be a useful ally.

Sending six cavalrymen ahead as scouts, Cortés marched into the country. After about ten miles, the scouts ran into an advance

party of about 15 warriors who attacked with spears, killing two horses, and wounding three others, as well as two horsemen. These were soon joined by some 4–5,000 warriors. The cavalry moved in and "did them some damage," and as soon as the infantry arrived, the Tlaxcalans withdrew.

After an uneasy night, fighting began again the next morning. This time, Cortés estimated there were as many as 100,000 warriors, who were held off by artillery, crossbows, musket fire, and cavalry until about an hour before sunset, when the Tlaxcalans again broke off. The Castilians retreated to a small hill, fortifying the temple they found on top. At dawn the next day Cortés led a raid that burned several small villages and brought their inhabitants back as prisoners. The Tlaxcalans responded by assaulting the hill with a force that Cortés estimated at about 149,000 men. Some managed to break the line, and the fighting turned to hand-to-hand combat, Toledo steel ranged against the razor-like stone weapons of the natives. Cortés continued with his dawn raids against the villages. This, together with the Castilian determination to hold the fort at any cost, was a new concept of war, and the Tlaxcalans were unsettled. Ultimately they sued for peace, explaining that they had attacked on the presumption that Cortés was allied with Mexico.

Tlaxcala, the Castilians learned, was bounded on all sides by Mexico and its allies. Indeed Moctezuma later told Andrés Tapia (a conquistador who wrote an account of the conquest in 1545) that the only reason he tolerated the country's existence was that it served as a convenient training ground for young warriors in the "flower wars" that brought enemy captives to Mexico for sacrifice. Economically it was also at the mercy of Mexico, because it had few resources and produced little, and was therefore reduced to bartering with its more powerful neighbor. Nevertheless, its warriors were numerous and well organized. Recognizing its potential as an ally, Cortés was careful to emphasize Castilian friendship. Arriving at the city of Tlaxcala, he quartered his men and staked out a sort of military reservation, the limits of which the soldiers were not to cross without permission.

The Tlaxcalan alliance proved to be a turning point in the Conquest, for without their massive military power, it is doubtful that a handful of Europeans and Totonac auxiliaries could have defeated Mexico. Tlaxcala remained faithful to the end, and throughout the colonial period was described in Spanish sources as "most loyal." This has earned the modern city and state the disdain of other parts of Mexico, particularly Mexico City, where citizens contend that the

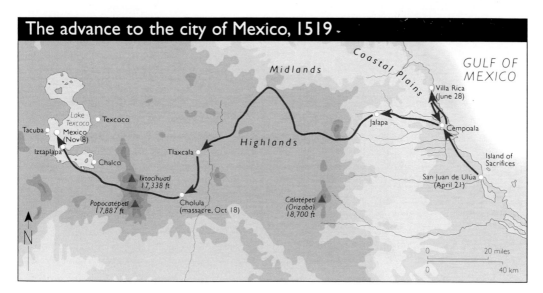

The advance to the city of Mexico, 1519

The temple at Cempoala, just one example of the spectacular architecture that amazed the conquistadors. (©Philip Baird www.anthroarcheart.org)

country was betrayed by Tlaxcala. Modern Tlaxcalans, however, are equally touchy about their reasons for siding with Cortés, and are quick to point out all the grievances their country had with Aztec Mexico.

By Cortés's own account, he spent 20 days in Tlaxcala, when the Mexican emissaries suggested he continue on another 30 or so miles to Cholula, a wealthy, populous trading city allied with Mexico. There, they told him, he could wait and learn whether or not Moctezuma would receive him. The Tlaxcalans were against the idea, claiming it was a trap. Moctezuma, they told him, had withdrawn troops from their own borders to strengthen the garrison at Cholula. The main road had been closed, and an alternative path had been constructed, full of pitfalls with sharpened stakes, to neutralize the cavalry. They also pointed out that no

neared Cholula, he sent most of the auxiliaries home, keeping only 5–6,000 men who were ordered to remain outside of the city, at the request of the Cholulans.

Cholula was a place of pilgrimage. At the time of the Conquest, it had 365 temples, one for each day of the Aztec year, and afterwards churches were said to have been built on each of them. Whether the church-to-temple ratio is entirely accurate is debatable, but modern Cholula must certainly have one of the highest densities of churches in relation to available real estate of any city in Mexico. Then and now, the city was dominated by the Tepanapa, a great temple that remains the largest single free-standing structure on earth.

The Cholulans welcomed the expedition with great ceremony, and provided comfortable quarters. Nevertheless, Cortés was suspicious because en route he had verified much of what the Tlaxcalans had told him. The attitude of the Cholulans, likewise, cooled. Over the next three days, food gradually worsened until, on the third day, it was stopped entirely. Visits by the local dignitaries became less frequent, until they also ceased. Crowds outside the quarters began to jeer and taunt the Castilians. The ever-vigilant doña Marina had struck up friendships among the noblewomen, and learned that a massacre was being prepared. This was confirmed by runners from the Tlaxcalans, who, from their camp, had observed events with growing uneasiness.

Cortés summoned the Cholulan leaders and, after hinting that he knew of the plot, said he wanted men as bearers for the trip into Mexico. When the bearers arrived, they were heavily armed and were, in fact, the elite of the warriors. Now convinced beyond all doubt, Cortés again assembled the Cholulans and deployed his men, telling them that when they heard a musket shot, they were to fall on the Cholulans outside the quarters. When the leaders arrived, they were taken into a courtyard and surrounded. Several were interrogated and confessed to the trap. The signal was given and the slaughter began. Having dispatched those

delegation from Cholula had come to visit, whereas those of more distant cities had. Cortés, however, remained adamant. He later admitted to the king that part of his determination was to impress the Tlaxcalans themselves, fearing that any hesitancy might show weakness; he was determined to convince all potential enemies and allies of Castilian invincibility. When the Tlaxcalans saw Cortés could not be dissuaded, they insisted on sending 100,000 well-armed warriors. Cortés assented, although, as his force around their quarters, the Castilians and the Totonac auxiliaries moved out into the city from house to house, hunting down and killing any warrior or potential warrior they could find. Several priests fled to the top of the Tepanapa, but died when the Castilians set the temple ablaze. Cortés estimated about 3,000 men were killed in the first two hours.

With the city in complete chaos, he now brought in their ancient enemies, the Tlaxcalans, and allowed them two days of pillage and slaughter. The inhabitants who survived the initial assault fled into the countryside. After several days, they came wandering back into Cholula, begging for mercy. Having made an example of anyone else who might oppose him, Cortés now relented and allowed them to return, promising his protection henceforth.

That Castilian account is different from that of the Mexicans. Sahagún's informants contend that the massacre was instigated by the Tlaxcalans, and make no mention of a plot by the Cholulans. This is unlikely, however, given Cortés's basic preference for diplomacy, with armed conflict as a last resort. Whatever the case, the news of the massacre shocked Moctezuma and his court; it was the exact opposite of what they had expected. He had intended for the Cholulans to finish the Castilians, but Cortés anticipated this, and hit first. Once more, the emperor sent emissaries with gifts, this time, however, with a double who would pass himself off as the emperor in a meeting with Cortés.

While the court worried, Cortés prepared for the final thrust to the city of Mexico. The skyline over Cholula is dominated by two giant volcanoes, Popocatépetl and Ixtacíhuatl, each more than 17,000 feet tall, rising above the mountains to the west. Popocatépetl, which began a new surge of eruptions in the late 1990s, likewise was active in 1519, and Cortés sent a detachment of soldiers to investigate. At 13,000 feet, they discovered a pass between the mountains and determined from local Indians that a good road led from the pass into the Valley of Mexico. They attempted to climb the mountain, but were forced back short of the

summit by the winds, tremors, clouds of ash, and glaciers. Nevertheless, they brought back samples of ice and snow to prove that it existed in a tropical climate.

Departing Cholula, the expedition was met by more ambassadors who offered to lead the way into Mexico by a different road than the one between the mountains. The Tlaxcalans, however, were suspicious, because the proposed route was through

The massacre at Cholula, illustrated in a 19th-century history of Mexico. (Author's collection)

rough country, ideally suited for ambush. Going into camp, Cortés sent a detachment of soldiers with the ambassadors to scout that route, and Diego Ordaz with the Tlaxcalans to scout beyond the pass. The first group returned with news that the route was impassable. A day later, Ordaz and the Tlaxcalans returned with an incredible story. The conquistador Alonso de Aguilar later recalled Ordaz "had seen another new world of large cities and towers, and a sea, and in that sea a very large city, which indeed seemed frightening and awesome." This was the wealthy, powerful Aztec capital, situated on its island in Lake Texcoco.

Descending down onto the plain, they passed through various tributary provinces, whose leaders almost universally complained of Mexican oppression. Ambassadors were sent ahead to the various cities and provinces on the route, and alliances were formed. It became increasingly obvious that these foreigners were seen as liberators, not necessarily benign, but at least the lesser of evils. The Aztec Empire was falling apart, as the years of ruinous tribute and cruelty that had made it the greatest power in North America now worked against it. In Huexotzingo, the leaders warned Cortés that Moctezuma would allow them to enter the city, then, having trapped them inside, would massacre them. Similar warnings were given in Amecameca and elsewhere.

En route, they were met by the embassy that included Moctezuma's double and which brought 3,000 pesos in gold. The double (whom Cortés identified as a brother of the emperor), represented himself as Moctezuma, but, after consulting with the Tlaxcalans and Totonacs, Cortés informed him that he knew better. He told the representatives that his own king in Spain had personally dispatched him to visit the capital, meet with Moctezuma, and report back, and that he could not disobey. The march continued, while the embassy returned shamefaced, to report to their emperor.

Sahagún's Mexican informants told a tale illustrating how devastating the chain of events had become for Mexican morale. In one, last, desperate attempt to forestall the inevitable, Moctezuma sent necromancers and sorcerers out to try to ward off the Castilians by enchantment. En route, however, they met a traveler who seemed almost berserk with rage. "What does Moctezuma pretend to accomplish with your remedies against the Spaniards? He has realized late that they are determined to take his kingdom, whatever he possesses, and even his honor, because of the great tyrannies he has committed against his vassals! He hasn't reigned as a lord, but as a tyrant and a traitor!" The terrified sorcerers listened as the man continued to rant. "Turn

around and look at Mexico, and what will happen to her before many days have passed!" Obeying, they turned and saw the city in flames. As they attempted to answer, the stranger disappeared. They now realized that he was Tezcatlipoca, paramount of the gods. Knowing they and their city were doomed, they abandoned their mission. Listening to their report, Moctezuma knew his gods had abandoned him, and he was completely alone. He began preparations to receive the Castilians in the capital itself.

At Ayotzingo, the Castilians were met by Moctezuma's distant cousin, Cacama, king of Texcoco.[2] He arrived in the splendor befitting a ruler of the Triple Alliance, carried on a litter borne by eight lords of subordinate cities. When he met Cortés, he announced that he had been sent to personally conduct the expedition to the city of Mexico. Gifts were exchanged, and the prince, his entourage, the Castilians, and their auxiliaries began the march, crossing the great Cuitláhuac Causeway that separates Lake Chalco from Lake Xochimilco, and on to Itzapalapa, on the shores of Lake Texcoco itself. Here, the lords of Itzapalapa and Coyoacán, met them with tribute. After spending the night, they marched out onto the Iztapalapa Causeway, that led into the capital. Bernal Díaz recalled the scene:

"We went ahead on our causeway which is eight paces wide and goes directly to the city of Mexico without deviation. The whole width was so full of people that there was hardly room, some were going to Mexico, and others were leaving. We could hardly get through because the Indians who came to see us filled the towers and cúes [temples] and came in canoes from every part of the lake. And it was not surprising because they had never seen horses, nor men like us. And when we saw such wonderful things we did not know what to say, or whether what we saw before us was real. On the land there were great cities, and on the lake many more. We saw the whole lake was filled with canoes, and at intervals on the causeway there were many bridges. Before us was the great city of Mexico. We had barely 400

2 The old accounts say "Cacamatzin," which means Lord Cacama.

soldiers, and we remembered the words and advice given us by the people of Guaxocinco [Huexotingo] and Tlaxcala and Tamanalco, and many others that we should beware of entering Mexico, because they would kill us once they had us inside." (Historia Verdadera)

Cacama and the other princes had gone ahead to prepare for the meeting between Cortés and Moctezuma. The emperor himself arrived on a litter with his brother, Cuitláhuac, prince of Iztapalapa, and Cacama on either side. Two hundred other princes formed the entourage, all of whom averted their eyes for they were forbidden to look at Moctezuma's face. A carpet was rolled out and Moctezuma stepped down on it, the two

Moctezuma. Illustration from a 19th-century history of Mexico. (Author's collection)

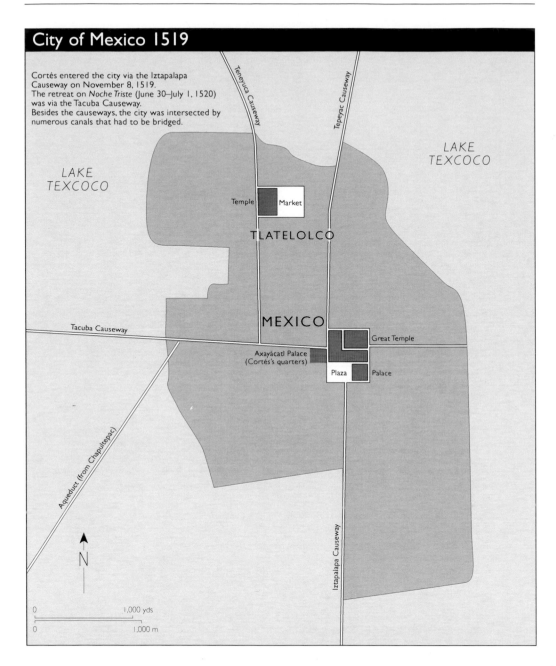

City of Mexico 1519

Cortés entered the city via the Iztapalapa
Causeway on November 8, 1519.
The retreat on *Noche Triste* (June 30–July 1, 1520)
was via the Tacuba Causeway.
Besides the causeways, the city was intersected by
numerous canals that had to be bridged.

LAKE TEXCOCO

LAKE TEXCOCO

Teneyuca Causeway

Tepeyac Causeway

Temple　Market

TLATELOLCO

MEXICO

Tacuba Causeway

Great Temple

Axayácatl Palace
(Cortés's quarters)

Plaza　Palace

Aqueduct (from Chapultepec)

Iztapalapa Causeway

N

0 　　　　1,000 yds
0 　　　　1,000 m

princes holding up his hands, while
attendants swept in front of him so that dust
would not touch his feet. Cortés started to
embrace him, but the princes indicated that
this was impossible. They did, however, allow
him to take a necklace from his own neck,
made of glass beads scented with musk,
interspersed with pearls, and put it around
the emperor's. Moctezuma summoned a
servant, who brought a packet which the

emperor opened. It contained a necklace
made of red snail shells, interspersed with
golden shrimp, which the emperor personally
place around Cortés's neck, to the
astonishment of his retainers. After an
exchange of pleasantries, Moctezuma ordered
Cacama and the prince of Iztapalapa to show
the Castilians to their quarters.

The Itzapalapa Causeway led into the very
center of the city which – then and now – is

Precinct of the Great Temple

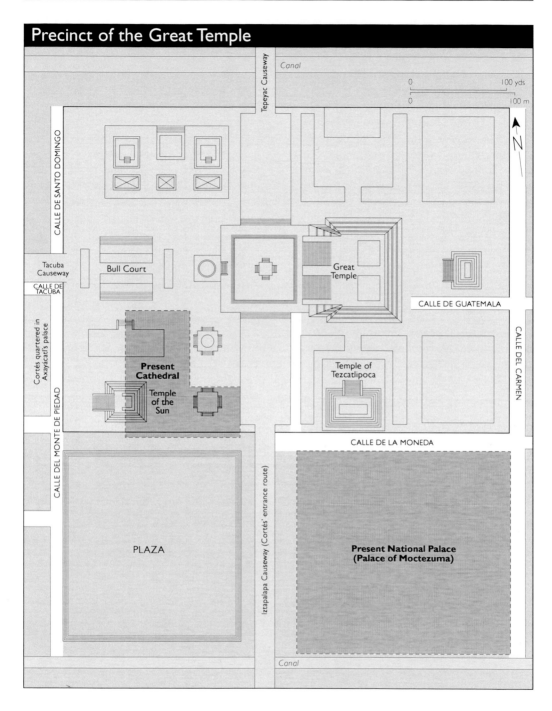

Tepeyac Causeway

Canal

0   100 yds
0   100 m

N

CALLE DE SANTO DOMINGO

Tacuba
Causeway

CALLE DE
TACUBA

Bull Court

Great
Temple

CALLE DE GUATEMALA

Cortés quartered in
Axayácatl's palace

Present
Cathedral

Temple
of the
Sun

Temple of
Tezcatlipoca

CALLE DEL CARMEN

CALLE DEL MONTE DE PIEDAD

CALLE DE LA MONEDA

Iztapalapa Causeway (Cortés' entrance route)

PLAZA

Present National Palace
(Palace of Moctezuma)

Canal

the administrative and spiritual center. It opened out onto a great plaza, now known as the Zócalo where crowds still gather for events and festivities of national importance. To the immediate east of the plaza was the palace of Moctezuma himself, now the site of the National Palace. North of the plaza were the temple precincts, now partly covered by the Metropolitan Cathedral, across from which are the ruins of the Great Temple itself. The Castilians were quartered in the palace of Moctezuma's father, Axayacatl, the site of which is to the immediate west of the Cathedral, and the immediate north of the modern Monte de Piedad (National Pawn Shop). Just north of this palace was the Tlacopán or Tacuba Causeway, which was to figure prominently in subsequent events.

Moctezuma was waiting in Axayacatl's palace when the Castilians arrived. Taking Cortés by the hand, the emperor led him to a throne, then took another next to it. Gifts of gold, silver, featherwork, and fine cotton garments were brought in. Then Moctezuma began to explain Mexican history, admitting to the fact that the Aztecs themselves were foreigners who had been brought to the region by a great chieftain. When that chieftain wanted to move on, however, the Aztecs had refused. The chieftain left for the east, but the Aztecs had always known that his descendants would return to rule over them. Now, it appeared the prophecy had been fulfilled. "And in all the land that lies in my domain, you may command as you will, for you shall be obeyed; and for all that we own is for you to dispose of as you choose," he said. He also mentioned that he knew the stories about him that the Tlaxcalans, Totonacs, and others had told, and cautioned Cortés not to take them too seriously. After telling the Castilians to make themselves at home, he departed.

The Castilians immediately set about organizing company quarters, siting their artillery, and assigning posts for infantry and cavalry. Once that was completed, they found the Mexicans had prepared a sumptuous banquet, and they ate it immediately. "And this," Bernal Díaz wrote, "was our daring and auspicious entrance into the great city of Tenustitán [Tenochititlán] Mexico, on the eighth day of the month of November, in the year of Our Savior Jesus Christ one thousand five hundred and nineteen. Thanks to Our Lord Jesus Christ for it all."

Disaster, then triumph

Acclimatization

For the next week, the Castilians were tourists. They were well housed and well fed, acquiring a taste for strange new things, such as chocolate (derived from the Nahuatl word *xocolatl*) whipped to a froth, corn tortillas, and chillis. Often they dined with the emperor, who entertained them with dancers, jugglers, and jesters, and introduced them to smoking after dinner. They saw the menagerie, with strange native animals such as the beautiful quetzal bird, whose long plumes adorned the headdresses of royalty, jaguars, and coyotes (which Bernal Díaz thought were jackals). Particularly repulsive to the European mind was a type of snake "that had on its tail something that sounds like bells," their first introduction to the rattlesnake. Writing of the menagerie with particular disgust, Díaz contended these animals were fed with the hearts and flesh of sacrificial victims.

They also saw the Great Temple, a massive pyramid surmounted by twin sanctuaries, dedicated to Huitzilopochtli, the peculiarly Aztec war god, and Tlaloc, the hideous, multi-fanged, goggle-eyed god of rain, passed down through millennia from one Mesoamerican culture to the next. These gods survived on the blood of sacrificial victims, who were bent backwards over small stones so that their chests were thrust upward, and their still-beating hearts ripped out by knife-wielding priests. Inside the dark, filthy sanctuaries were the idols which, according to Andrés Tapia, were smeared with blood to the depth of two or three fingers.

In front of the Temple was the *tzompantli*, the great rack where the heads of sacrificial victims were threaded on beams set between towers. The towers themselves also were made of skulls mortared together. Visiting the *tzompantli*, Tapia and Gonzalo de Umbría did some idle counting and multiplication, and determined there were 136,000 skulls on the beams themselves, not including those in the towers.

On the fourth day, Moctezuma invited the Castilians to accompany him to Tlatelolco, the commercial center of the empire. Although Mexican, Tlatelolco had established its independence early in the Aztec era, and remained separate until 1473, when Moctezuma's father, the Emperor Axyacatl, conquered it and made it into a borough of Mexico proper. Nevertheless, Tlatelolco maintained control of commerce, and had its own Great Temple complex, rivaling that of Mexico.

The vast market square, which virtually every Castilian chronicler agreed was more than double the size of the great square of Salamanca, was surrounded by a portico (the whole area was roughly 500 ft square). Everyday, at least 20,000 people were trading, and on the main market day, every fifth day, this number more than doubled. Each type of trade had its own area with the gold merchants in one, featherworkers in another, stoneworkers in another, slave dealers, traders in cotton, produce, game animals, medicinal roots, and every other imaginable item in its own area. Currency was feather quills filled with gold dust of a specific weight, or cacao beans. Some of the Castilian veterans, who had traveled as far as Constantinople, said they had never seen so large a market, nor one so well regulated.

Looming over the market was the Great Temple of Tlatelolco. Bernal Díaz counted 114 steps up the pyramid, from the top of which, they could see the entire city. There were three causeways into the city from the mainland, with bridges at regular intervals.

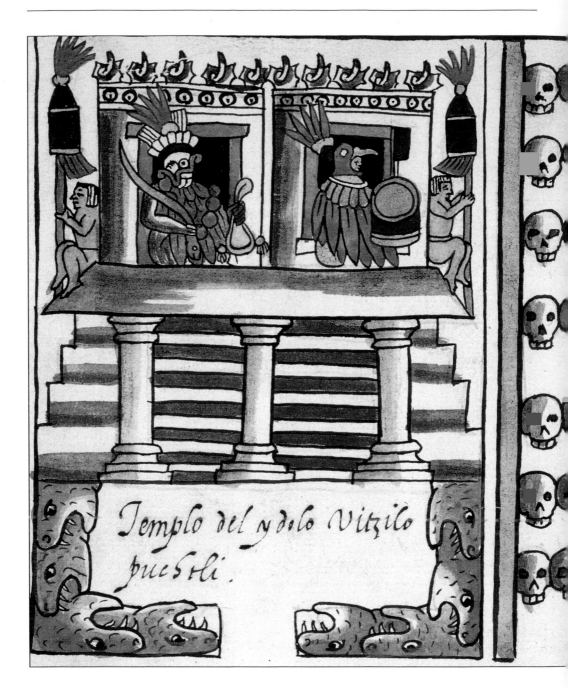

Templo del ydolo Vitzilo puesthi.

There was an aqueduct that brought in fresh water from springs at Chapultepec. The city itself was divided by canals traversed by drawbridge or canoe. In view of later events, one may surmise that Cortés noted everything, and committed it all to memory.

At Cortés's request, Moctezuma led them inside the sanctuary, dominated by an image of Huitzilopochtli, along with statues of Tezcatlipoca, the paramount god, and Xipe Totec, the flayed god of harvest. Díaz noted that, "All the walls of that oratory were bathed and black with encrusted blood, and the floors were the same, and it stank dreadfully, to which the butchers of Castile could not compare. And there had they offered five hearts sacrificed that day … They had a drum great in dimension, that when

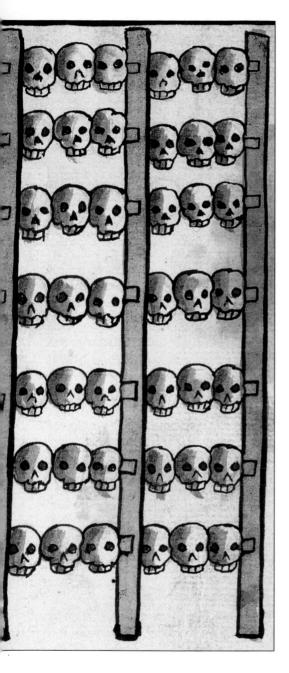

A contemporary depiction of the *Templo Mayor* (Great Temple) and the *tzompantli* (skull rack). The Spaniards found the temple imposing and regarded the sacrificial practices as repugnant. (John Carter Brown Museum)

had been burned to fumigate those idols, and the whole was such that I curse it, and it was clotted with blood, and stank like a slaughterhouse, and we could not wait until we left that stink and that horrible sight."

Turning to the emperor, Cortés said he could not understand how such a great and wise prince could not have realized that these were not gods but demons. In order that he and his priests might truly understand the nature of the idols, he asked to place a cross on top of the sanctuary, and inside, a statue of the Virgin "so that you may see the fear the idols have of her."

As this was translated, two priests glared malevolently, and Moctezuma angrily replied, "Lord Malinche, if I had believed that you would speak with such dishonor to my gods, I would not have brought you here. We have them because they are good, and they give us health, and rains, and good plantings and seasons, and victories when we want them, and we are required to worship and to sacrifice. And we pray that you do not say further words in their dishonor."

Smiling, Cortés suggested it was time to leave. Moctezuma agreed, but replied that he would have to stay, and pray and make sacrifices to ask pardon of the gods for bringing the Castilians. Cortés then said, "I ask my lord's pardon if this be so."

The emperor, however, was less intractable with regard to how the Castilians worshiped among themselves, and gave permission to set up a chapel in their quarters. As a room was being surveyed, the carpenter noticed a doorway that had recently been bricked up and plastered over. Cortés ordered the door forced open. Inside was a vast chamber containing the accumulated wealth of conquest and empire. After a quick conference between Cortés and the men present, it was decided to seal the door again, so that Moctezuma would not realize it had been discovered.

they beat it, it had a mournful sound of the style they say one hears from an instrument of the infernal regions, and one can hear it from two leagues distant; they say the drumheads are made from the skins of great serpents.

And in that place they had various things diabolical to see: bugles and trumpets and sacrificial knives, and many hearts of Indians

Imprisonment of Moctezuma

Cortés, and some of the more experienced captains and soldiers were worried. Fabulous as it was, the treasure had impressed them with the might and power of the Aztec empire. They were beginning to see the city as a trap. Moctezuma could stop their food and water, raise the bridges, then set hordes of warriors on them. Their fears seemed confirmed when runners from the coast brought word of a rebellion, instigated by the Mexicans, against the garrison at Villa Rica. The Tlaxcalans also reported that Moctezuma planned to raise the bridges in the city. Cortés decided the time had come to act. Taking a squad of armed soldiers, he called on the emperor, accused him of treachery, and placed him under arrest. Moctezuma argued for an hour but, overpowered by the personality of Cortés, and with a not-too-veiled threat from doña Marina, he acquiesced, and was conveyed back to the Castilian quarters in Axayacatl's palace. The population was given to understand that Moctezuma had taken up residence there, and Cortés allowed the usual functions of government to continue, but under guard and with doña Marina always listening.

On the summons of Moctezuma, Cualpopoca, the Mexican governor of the Pánuco region, who had instigated the uprising, was summoned to Mexico. Arriving about mid-December on a rich litter attended by his sons and 15 nobles, Cualpopoca was arrested, and together with his entourage, was handed over to Cortés, who ordered them interrogated under torture. They confessed, and implicated Moctezuma. They were burned at the stake in the great square, where López de Gómara wrote that the local population watched silently, too terrified to interfere. Cortés ordered Moctezuma chained.

It was increasingly obvious that Moctezuma was completely cowed by the Castilians. Others, however, were not. Chief among them was Cacama, king of Texcoco, the second partner in the Mexican Triple Alliance. Initially, he had urged Moctezuma to resist the Castilians, and when it became obvious he would not, he decided the time had come to seize power and expel the foreigners. He was joined in the conspiracy by Moctezuma's brother, Cuitláhuac, prince of Itzapalapa, and several of the other more important vassal states in the Valley of Mexico. Moctezuma learned of the plot, and by now completely in thrall to Cortés, arranged for some of the still-loyal nobles to seize Cacama and bring him to Mexico, where he was turned over to the Castilians and placed under arrest. Cortés deposed him, replacing him as king of Texcoco with his brother, Coanacoch.

So far, Cortés had managed the expedition without a single serious error. Now, however, he overreached himself. Wily and sophisticated as he was, he was nevertheless driven partly by his religious convictions and believed that the time had come to throw down the idols of Mexico, end the sacrifices and impose the rule of the Catholic Church. With a hand-picked squad he crossed the compound to the Great Temple of Mexico, and climbed the steps of the pyramid. Reaching the platform, the soldiers drew their swords and slashed through a heavy curtain decorated with bells that hid the sanctuary. The racket brought the priests running and found Cortés inside, looking at the blood-soaked idols and muttering "Oh God! Why do You permit such great honor paid the Devil in this land? Look with favor, Lord, upon our service to You here."

Turning to the priests, he told them the gods would be replaced by a statue of the Virgin and Child and the walls would be whitewashed. They laughed and replied that these were gods not only of the city, but of the entire empire. The people were willing to die for them, and upon seeing the Castilians mount the pyramid, some already began preparations for a rebellion. Angered, Cortés sent one of the men back to the palace to strengthen the guard around Moctezuma and send a detail of 30 or 40 men to the Temple. Then, as Andrés Tapia recalled:

"On my faith as a gentleman I swear by God that, as I recall it now, the marqués [Cortés] leaped supernaturally, and, balancing himself by gripping the bar in the middle, he reached as high as the idol's eyes and thus tore down the gold masks, saying: 'Something we must venture for the Lord'."

Moctezuma suspected what was about to happen, and demanded to be taken to the temple, where he confronted Cortés. Now it was the emperor's turn for subtlety, and he suggested that the Castilians leave the idols undisturbed, and erect a cross and the religious statues next to the Mexican gods. Cortés, meanwhile, had overcome his initial outrage and agreed, saying the idols were nothing but stone and therefore unimportant. However, he demanded the temple be cleansed and whitewashed, and the sacrifices end.

The violation of their gods was more than the people were willing to tolerate. The priests, seeing a threat to their massive power, spread the word that the two great gods, Huitzilopochtli and Tezcatlipoca, would abandon Mexico unless Christian symbols were removed from the temple, and the Castilians themselves destroyed. Cortés's page, Orteguilla, who had quickly learned Nahuatl, and to whom Moctezuma had taken a liking, reported that the emperor was quietly conferring with his generals. The Tlaxcalans and doña Marina also warned of an impending revolt. Even Moctezuma told Cortés that unless he evacuated his men and left the country, they would be destroyed.

Cortés now realized his diplomacy was spent, and he would have to hold the country by sheer force. He sent secret orders to the carpenters in Villa Rica to begin the construction of three ships to sail to the immediate Indies for reinforcements. Meanwhile, he stalled, telling Moctezuma that he and his men would like to return home, but were unable because they had no way of leaving the country. One day, however, Moctezuma advised him that he could now leave, because a fleet had anchored at Villa Rica. Cortés correctly surmised that this expedition came from Cuba, where Governor Velásquez had learned of his plans when the shipload of tribute had put in to reprovision for the trip back to Spain. He also knew that before Cualpopoca had instigated the uprising in the Pánuco, he had already expelled another expedition by Francisco de Garay, the governor of Jamaica.

Arrival of the Narváez expedition

The new expedition to Mexico was commanded by Pánfilo de Narváez, who had encountered one of Cortés's scouting parties, and learned of the situation in Mexico. Unable to occupy Villa Rica, where the tough, defiant captain Gonzalo Sandoval dug in for a siege, Narváez bypassed the town and continued on to Cempoala, where he was now quartered with his troops. Sandoval had also arrested three of Narváez's envoys and sent them under guard to Mexico, where Cortés learned of his adversary's strength. Letters from Narváez, calling Cortés's men "bandits" and "traitors," and threatening them with death, were read out to the Castilians in Mexico to stir them up against the newcomers. Then the envoys were sent back to Narváez, loaded with gifts and stories of the wealth and grandeur that Cortés offered, compared to their own lack of prospects with Narváez. Finally, Cortés set out for the coast with 250 picked men, leaving Pedro de Alvarado in command of the city.

There can be little doubt that the new arrivals were swayed by the gifts of gold and talk of riches. Yet one must also remember that they had only recently arrived from the comparative luxury of Cuba. No doubt they also would have noticed the lean, leathery countenances of Cortés's men, and their battered armor, and realized they would be facing battle-hardened veterans. The Narváez expedition was effectively defeated even before it fought.

The battle itself occurred at Cempoala on May 27, 1520. Cortés moved in before dawn in a driving rain, which his own men, accustomed to hardship, barely noticed, but which drove Narváez's men under cover. The veterans quickly seized the artillery and unhorsed the cavalry, and rushed into the city. Much of the resistance came from the main temple, where Narváez fortified himself with crossbowmen and musketeers. They mounted a counterattack, but at that moment, Sandoval arrived with a detachment from the coast, and the combined forces pushed them back. Then the roof of the temple was set on fire, driving Narváez's men out. Narváez himself, badly wounded and having lost an eye in the fighting, was sent back to the coast as a prisoner. A detachment was sent to Villa Rica to remove the rudders, compasses, and sails of the ships, so they could not escape to Cuba. The bulk of Narváez's men, having accepted a pardon from Cortés, were rearmed and incorporated into the army.

As he prepared to return to Mexico, Cortés little realized he was leaving behind an unexpected and invisible ally that would have devastating consequences for the native people. An African slave attached to Narváez's men had smallpox, and infected the household where he was quartered in Cempoala. As López de Gómara noted, "it spread from one Indian to another, and they, being so numerous and eating and sleeping together, quickly infected the whole country."

The people of the Old World, over hundreds of generations and perhaps millions of deaths, had built a resistance to the disease. The genetically weak died off; the genetically strong recovered and procreated descendants with enhanced immune systems. The people of the New World had never experienced smallpox and had no inherited immunity. It is estimated that as much as 90 percent of the entire native population of the New World ultimately died of diseases introduced after Columbus.

In modern times, the science of microbiology has diminished the impact of disease and it is impossible for the 21st century imagination to truly comprehend the impact of a pandemic. The elders die before they can impart their accumulated wisdom. The priests, philosophers, and political leaders die, taking with them their belief structure, knowledge, and governmental institutions. Craftsmen, farmers, and warriors die. Children are orphaned. Often the dead outnumber the living, and the streets are filled with decaying corpses, exacerbating the crisis. Society quite simply collapses. As much as any other factor, this new and unknown plague would decide the outcome of the Conquest.

The Toxcatl massacre

While Cortés was dealing with Narváez, Alvarado had problems of his own back in Mexico. May, which the Aztecs called Toxcatl, was sacred to Tezcatlipoca, and the occasion of great festivals, during which a proxy for the god was sacrificed. Alvarado gave permission for the celebration on condition that the Christian symbols in the temple were not disturbed, and there would be no sacrifices. A few days before the ceremony was to begin, however, he inspected the temple, found fresh sacrifices, and slaves awaiting their turn. Freeing the slaves, he arrested several priests who, on interrogation, admitted arms were stored in the temple precincts, and confessed that on the completion of the ceremony, the Castilian guards would be overwhelmed and the cross thrown down as the signal for an uprising. It would be all the easier because the city was filled with pilgrims who were outraged at the sight of the cross on the temple and by its foreign guards.

Alvarado waited for the ceremony to begin on May 18, then, leaving part of his troops in the palace, he took the rest into the temple compound, pushing his way through the crowd. The procession of priests

Pedro de Alvarado (1485–1541). Headstrong and impulsive, Alvarado may have provoked the uprising in the city of Mexico by overreacting. Nevertheless, in any crisis, he was valiant, decisive, and loyal to the end. (Topham Picturepoint)

parted to reveal armed warriors, but Alvarado was expecting this, and his men charged. Ignoring the rank and file, they went for the nobles and warlords, slaughtering the leadership and leaving the masses of warriors in confusion. Meanwhile, about 1,000 Tlaxcalans surrounded the temple court and held off reinforcements. Together, Alvarado and the Tlaxcalans fought their way back to the palace, leaving the compound littered with corpses and drenched in blood.

Couriers brought word to Cortés that the city was in rebellion, Alvarado was under siege, and by now in danger of collapse. He rushed his newly strengthened army back through Tlaxcala, picking up several thousand more auxiliaries. The closer he came to the capital, the more signs he saw of rebellion. There were no welcoming delegations and the people were sullen. A quiet reigned over the city as the force arrived on the evening of June 24. There were accusations and counter-accusations between Alvarado and Moctezuma. Cortés tended to believe Moctezuma's account, and Alvarado received a thorough dressing-down. Nevertheless, Moctezuma also received his share of wrath, because Cortés had learned the emperor had been conspiring secretly with Narváez.

The arguments quickly became academic because the Mexicans renewed the siege. Hordes of warriors rushed the palace, their sheer numbers rendering artillery, musket fire, and crossbows ineffective. Dozens dropped with every charge, but still more came, forcing their way into the palace and setting it on fire in several places. Finally, they were pushed back by sword point. The Castilians next built siege towers in an effort to capture some of the surrounding buildings that Mexican slingers and archers were using as vantage points. When these failed, Cortés led a raiding party that captured and burned the temple, although the Christian images had already been removed by the Mexicans themselves. After that he began leading parties out into the city to burn the surrounding buildings. Nevertheless, it was becoming obvious that ultimately the Mexicans would prevail by sheer numbers.

Almost every soldier was wounded in some way. In the midst of the fighting, the Mexican electors deposed Moctezuma, and named Cuitláhuac emperor.

Late in the siege Moctezuma died, although the exact cause will never be known. Cortés contended that the former emperor went out to address the crowd in an effort to end the fighting. When he reached a breastworks he was struck on the head by a stone, and died of the injury three days later. The Mexicans, however, told a different story. Durán's informants said the wound from the stone had healed, and that he was murdered by the Castilians. Sahagún was told that Moctezuma did address the crowd, which only infuriated them more. After that, Cortés decided he was a liability, and ordered him garroted along with several other nobles, and the bodies thrown down from the roof of the palace.

The native version of events, that the emperor was murdered by the Castilians, tends to be accepted by historians of the modern, post-colonial era. Yet the fact is that virtually every conquistador account upholds Cortés, and some of these soldiers-turned-writers had no particular reason for doing so unless it was the truth. The two most convincing are Alonso de Aguilar, and Bernal Díaz. When Aguilar wrote his memoir, he was past 80, and living in menial servitude as a Dominican under the religious name of Fra Francisco, in an apparent effort to atone for his own atrocities during the Conquest. He stated that Moctezuma died of the head injury, although he admits that Cortés had the other prisoners murdered. Díaz, who admired Moctezuma, wrote that after he was stoned by the crowd, the emperor became despondent, refusing food and medical treatment. Considering that Moctezuma had been assaulted by a population which only recently had considered him a demigod, Díaz's scenario is most believable, although his remark that the Castilians wept over his death is, at the very least, an exaggeration.

By June 30, with the siege six days old, the leading captains and the rank and file realized their position in the city was untenable. If they remained, they would be massacred.

When Cortés demurred, the captains, including the normally loyal Alvarado brothers, came as close to mutiny as they ever would during the Conquest, informing him that he could either lead them out or stay behind. Accepting the inevitable, Cortés agreed and began laying plans for a retreat that would commence at midnight that very night.

Breakout and retreat

It was at this point that Aguilar reports Moctezuma's death, and Cortés ordered the slaughter of the remaining chiefs. Then, with nothing more to gain by concealment, the great treasure room was broken open, and about eight tons of gold, silver, and gems parceled out. One-fifth went to the Crown, according to law, and one-fifth to Cortés himself, according to the old agreement back in Villa Rica, by which he "accepted" the position to which the men "appointed" him. The bulk of this was melted down and turned into ingots for ease of transportation. Seven wounded war horses and a mare, along with 80 Tlaxcalan bearers were provided for the king's share. Once these formalities were completed, the rest was turned over to the men in a free-for-all. The bulk of it was grabbed by the Narváez men, while most of Cortés's veterans contented themselves with small, light gemstones or other trinkets that weighed little. Unlike the newcomers, they knew what they were up against, and that, with or without treasure, they would be very lucky to come out alive. Bales of quetzal feathers, priceless to the Indians, were distributed among the Tlaxcalans.

Carpenters ripped out beams from the palace, and put together a portable bridge to throw over the gaps in the causeway. At midnight, the long line of Spaniards and Indian auxiliaries filed out along the Tacuba Causeway. The weather turned ugly and a rainstorm broke, driving many of the Mexican sentries under cover. Then came one of those freak occurrences that so often change the course of events. According to some sources, a woman left her home to draw water, saw them, and gave the alarm. According to others, it was a sentry. Either way, within minutes, the great temple drum sounded, stirring the city to action. Warriors swarmed onto the causeway, and more came up alongside in canoes. The Mexicans' loathing of the Castilians was so strong that they seem to have ignored their usual mode of war, and attempted to kill rather than capture their enemies. In his own picturesque style, Bernal Díaz recalled them shouting, "Oh, villains, do you still live?"

"Here many Spaniards fell," Aguilar wrote, "some dead and some wounded, and others without any injury who fainted away from fright. And since all of us were fleeing, there was not a man who would lift a hand to help his companion or even his own father, nor a brother his own brother."

Muskets and crossbows, useless in close quarters, were thrown aside as men relied on sword thrusts to get through. A rearguard with the baggage was cut off, and the men retreated up the steps of the temple for a last stand, where they were finally overpowered. Many of the Mexicans fell to plundering the baggage train, giving the remnants of the army a breather as it made its way across the lake to the safety of the mainland.

Modern authorities estimate Spanish losses to be at least 600, the bulk of the army. The Tlaxcalan loss was several thousand. The night of June 30/July 1, 1520 is known in Mexican history as the *Noche Triste*, the "Sad Night."

The battle of Otumba

The battered, beaten Castilians dragged their way back toward Tlaxcala, more or less constantly harassed by skirmishers. Finally, the Mexicans decided to destroy them completely and finish the war. The place picked for the final blow was the plain of Otumba, near the sacred ruins of Teotihuacán where, it was presumed, their massed infantry would overwhelm the remnants of Cortés's army. In choosing this ground they committed a fatal error. Their

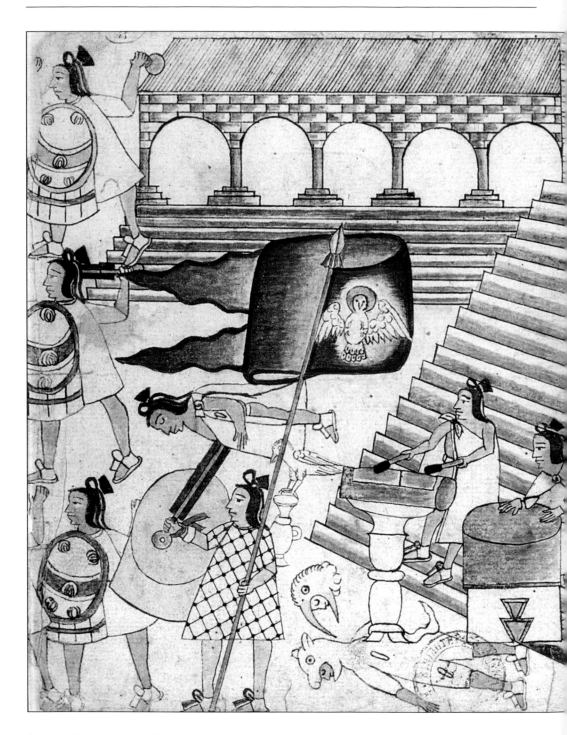

firsthand experience with the great
Andalusian war horses was within the city
and on the bridges, where the horses'
iron-shod hooves slipped on the pavement,
and their mobility was restricted. They had
completely underestimated them, and now

presented Cortés with the perfect situation
for cavalry.

The battle, which was fought on July 7,
was very close. According to Alonso de
Aguilar, Cortés was in tears as he exhorted
the men for one final effort. Recounting the

Mexican warriors defending the Great Temple. One has a captured Spanish standard. From the *Codex Azcatitlan*, Plate 24. (Ann Ronan Picture Library)

we were exhausted and nearly all of us wounded and weak from hunger." Finally, Cortés spotted the group of warlords directing the battle and, lining up his lancers, led a mounted charge through the massed warriors, the horses breaking through the mass of warriors to the warlords. The senior chief was impaled on a lance and the Mexicans, on the verge of victory, lost their morale and began to retreat.

The army was saved, but was in no condition to do anything but continue on to Tlaxcala. Bernal Díaz estimated that besides the European losses on the *Noche Triste*, another 72 had died in the fighting since, along with five Spanish women who had come with Narváez. The heaviest losses, in fact, were among the Narváez people, who were unaccustomed to the life-or-death nature of the war, and to the discipline necessary to stay alive, and who had been weighted down with treasure on the bridges.

The Mexicans had already approached the Tlaxcalans and asked them to put aside the old grievances and unite against the foreigners, and one faction in Tlaxcala was amenable. The senior lords, however, quelled this movement at its inception, determined to remain steadfast to Cortés, and warned of dire consequences against whoever sided with Mexico. Thus, when the exhausted, battered Spaniards arrived in Tlaxcala on July 10, they were greeted with the words, "This is your home, where you may rest and find pleasure after the hardships you have suffered."

The Conquest revived

Despite his defeat, Cortés was determined to go back, finish with Mexico, and subjugate the entire country. In this, he was backed by his old veterans. After sending to Villa Rica for more powder and arms, resting his men, and allowing them to recuperate from their wounds, he sent an expeditionary force of

struggle for King Charles, Cortés himself wrote, "We could hardly distinguish between ourselves and them, so fiercely and closely did they fight with us. Certainly we believed that it was our last day, for the Indians were very strong and we could resist but feebly, as

The Temple of the Sun at Teotihuacan, seen here from a ceremonial complex known as "the Citadel," was already ancient when the Aztecs first arrived in the Valley of Mexico as semi-barbaric nomads. They made this temple the center of their world and the mythical point of their origin. (©Philip Baird www.anthroarcheart.org)

Spaniards and Tlaxcalans to subjugate the city of Tepeaca, where the Mexican garrison met him on a plain and, as at Otumba, was cut to pieces by the cavalry. With this boost to morale, and with the discipline it instilled in the Narváez contingent, he moved again against various other Mexican towns, sacking some and frightening others into submission.

Having subjugated the entire province, Cortés founded the city Segura de la Frontera, to use as a base against Mexico. A complete administration was established, and buildings and fortifications erected in a remarkably short time. The site was chosen not only for its strategic position, but because the countryside was ideally suited for future settlement. As ever, Cortés was looking ahead. Some of his men were less enthusiastic, and he had to quell a potential mutiny among some of the Narváez hardliners, hanging one of their ringleaders.

Sailors and carpenters had been summoned from Villa Rica with the equipment from the destroyed fleet. They began building 13 brigantines that would be disassembled, hauled in pieces overland, and reassembled on the lake. Cortés was leaving nothing to chance.

The old luck was returning. Two ships put in from Cuba, unaware of the turn of events, bringing arms, powder and equipment for Narváez. Cortés requisitioned them, and appropriated the men and equipment from two ships sent from Jamaica to reprovision Governor Garay's ill-fated ventures. He sent four ships to Hispaniola to bring horses and men. Having determined that swordsmanship alone was not enough, he procured horses, firearms, crossbows, and powder from Santo Domingo. Finally, the bribe sent to the king in the earliest days of the expedition began to pay off, as arms, equipment, and men began arriving from Spain itself.

As he prepared for the advance, Cortés promulgated a series of orders:

● No one should blaspheme Christ, the Virgin Mary, the Apostles, or the Saints.

- No soldier should mistreat or rob the Indian auxiliaries.
- No soldier should depart from camp for any reason.
- All soldiers should wear good armor (the native armor that many had adopted was to be well quilted), and should wear a neck guard, helmet, and leggings, and carry a shield.
- No soldier should gamble over a horse or arms.
- Unless sick or wounded, all soldiers were to sleep fully armed and shod, and ready for battle, in case of night attack.
- Sleeping on guard duty, or leaving a post was punishable by death.
- Going from one camp to another without permission was punishable by death.
- Desertion in battle was punishable by death.

Meanwhile, the city of Mexico was suffering a different scourge. Smallpox had worked its way over the mountains and entered the valley through Chalco, devastating the capital for 60 days. Among the dead was the Emperor Cuitláhuac, who was succeeded by a cousin, Cuauhtémoc. Although only 25, his resistance in the final days of the empire would elevate him in the Mexican mind as the greatest of all the emperors and, in modern times, as a symbol of nationalism and independence.

The siege of Mexico, 1521

On December 26, 1520 Cortés marched out of Segura de la Frontera. Besides the well-equipped, reinforced European contingent, he had 10,000 Tlaxcalan auxiliaries, and the leaders of Tlaxcala promised more as needed. They crossed the mountains and entered Texcoco unopposed, where they established quarters, and smashed the idols in the temples. Expeditionary forces were sent to the surrounding towns, and many surrendered. Representatives of other towns said they would surrender except for the Mexican

garrisons. Occasionally, they would skirmish with Mexican troops. After one particularly fierce fight, Xochimilco fell, and once again Cortés stood on the shores of the lake with the city of Mexico visible in the distance.

To avoid a protracted siege, Cortés sent peace overtures to Cuauhtémoc. When these were refused, he subjugated the towns around the lake to secure the mainland for a blockade. A company under Gonzalo de Sandoval captured a dependency of Texcoco where they found the flayed faces of two Spaniards, captured during the *Noche Triste* and sacrificed in the temple. The skin was tanned with the beards intact. Other offerings included four horsehides, complete with hooves and shoes, and the clothing of the Spaniards who had been sacrificed. In one of the cages where the victims were held while they waited the knife, a member of the Narváez expedition, Juan Yuste, had scratched his name.

On April 28, the brigantines were launched on Lake Texcoco. Messengers were sent to Tlaxcala, Cholula, Huexotzingo, and other allied states, and within a week the auxiliaries began arriving in Texcoco. Fifty thousand came from Tlaxcala alone, parading into the city with their battle standards, and shouting, "Castile! Castile! Tlaxcala! Tlaxcala!" With the city of Mexico blockaded, Cortés finalized his plans. Alvarado would lead 30 cavalrymen, 18 crossbowmen, 150 infantry, and 25,000 Tlaxcalans from Tacuba. Olíd would attack from Coyoacán with 33 cavalry, 18 crossbowmen, 160 infantry, and 20,000 native auxiliaries. Sandoval would lead 24 cavalrymen, four musketeers, 13 crossbowmen, 150 infantry, and 30,000 auxiliaries from Itzapalapa. Cortés himself would command the fleet, with each ship carrying a captain, six crossbowmen or musketeers, and 12 oarsmen. The aqueduct carrying fresh water from Chapultepec was cut, and the city was now isolated.

Cortés and his captains began an inspection of the causeways. They ordered some broken sections to be filled so that cavalry might pass, but ahead they saw more breaks and barricades.

The Castilian retreat after the *Noche Triste*

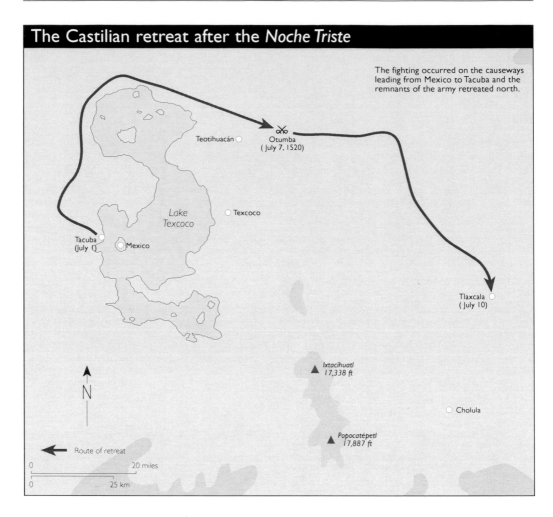

The fighting occurred on the causeways leading from Mexico to Tacuba and the remnants of the army retreated north.

Teotihuacán

Otumba
(July 7, 1520)

Lake
Texcoco

Texcoco

Tacuba
(July 0

Mexico

Tlaxcala
(July 10)

Ixtacihuatl
17,338 ft

N

Cholula

Popocatépetl
17,887 ft

← Route of retreat

0   20 miles

0   25 km

On May 31, 1521 Sandoval started out for Itzapalapa to secure the causeway and begin attacking the city. Cortés boarded one of the brigantines and began moving to support Sandoval from the lake. After securing a fortified hill that commanded the water, he turned the ships toward Mexico, where he encountered about 500 canoes loaded with warriors. A fresh breeze blew in from the mainland, the sails filled, and the Castilian fleet smashed through the canoes, wrecking many and drowning the warriors, and driving the rest back to the city. The siege of Mexico had begun.

The next 80 days were desperate. The Castilians fought their way yard by yard along the causeways, only to be pushed back and forced to retake the same ground. On the Tacuba Causeway, the site of which is now covered by a broad avenue called Puente de Alvarado (Alvarado's Bridge), Alvarado rashly made a dash to capture the temple precincts. The Mexicans retreated, leaving behind a gap in the causeway of about 60 feet. Alvarado and the cavalry rode into the water and came up on the other side of the break, while the infantry began filling in the gap. Suddenly, canoes swarmed into it, closing a carefully prepared ambush. The brigantines rushed to help, but were wedged up against a barrier of stakes driven into the lake bed just below the surface. Alvarado managed to fight his way back, but five men had been taken alive.

Capture meant sacrifice. Often in the distance, the Castilians heard the mournful sound of the great temple drum, the conch shell trumpets, and other horns signifying the brutal sacrifice of their comrades. As they

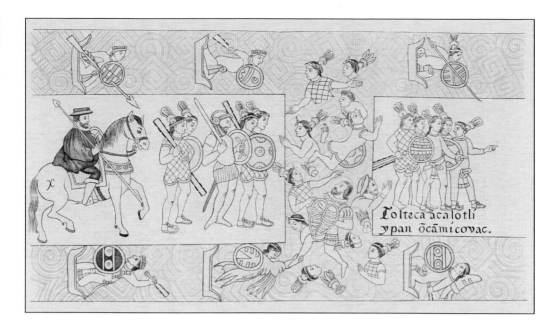

Cortés and the Tlaxcalans battle their way along a causeway into the city of Mexico. The scene shows the desperate fighting that occurred in gaps in the bridge. From the *Lienzo de Tlaxcala*, Plate 18. (American Museum of Natural History)

pushed farther into the city, and closer to the temple, they could actually see the ceremony on the great platform atop the pyramid, but could do nothing but pray. The soldiers adopted the habit of closing each day of battle with the prayer, "Oh, thanks be to God that they did not carry me off today for sacrifice." As more and more of their companions were dragged to the stones and slaughtered, their hatred of the Mexicans increased. Just as no quarter was expected, none was given.

In battle the Mexicans tried to demoralize the Tlaxcalans and other auxiliaries by throwing the stewed limbs of sacrificial victims into their ranks, shouting, "Eat the flesh of these *tueles* [gods – a reference to the near divine status in which the Castilians were first held] and of your brothers, because we are sated with it . . ."

Cortés now ordered a temporary halt, sending small details into the city to maintain the semblance of an offensive. His men had been fighting almost constantly for ten weeks, and the allied states were becoming unnerved at the Mexican tenacity. The uneasiness increased as couriers from Mexico slipped through the blockade and displayed European body parts as trophies of battle and sacrifice. Castilian troops had to be detached from the main body, and sent around to the allied cities to suitably impress their leaders and keep them in line. The point was made, and when Cortés renewed the offensive in late July, he had 150,000 Indian auxiliaries. He now began a policy of devastation. As each block of the city was secured, he demolished the buildings and used them to fill the canals and gaps in the causeways to provide a level field for his soldiers and horses. To make matters worse, the people of Xochimilco, Cuitláhuac, and Itzapalapa now were making raids of their own, crossing the lake in canoes, plundering and carrying off women and children. Although Cuauhtémoc managed to stop it, the division of his forces between these pirate raids and the Castilian assault seriously hampered his defense.

The city itself was a shambles, and the people were suffering. Already weakened by the recent smallpox epidemic, and with food and water cut off by the blockade, they were dying in great numbers. Alonso de Aguilar

Detail showing the intricate carved and gilt design on the back of a wooden spear-thrower. (Ann Ronan Picture Library)

wrote, "[T]here was a great pestilence in the city because there were so many people there, especially women, and they had nothing more to eat. We soldiers could scarcely get about the streets because of the Indians who were sick from hunger, pestilence and smallpox." Many noncombatants were coming to the Spanish lines to give themselves up.

Whatever the atrocities for which the Castilians may be blamed in the five centuries since the Conquest, their acts paled in comparison to those of their Tlaxcalan allies. Centuries of hate and the basic viciousness of Mesoamerican warfare combined in a violence that appalled even Cortés himself. As he later wrote to the king:

"[W]e had more trouble in preventing our allies from killing with such cruelty than we had in fighting the enemy. For no race, however savage, has ever practiced such fierce and unnatural cruelty as the natives of these parts. Our allies also took many spoils that day, which we were unable to prevent, as they numbered more than 150,000 and we Spaniards were only some nine hundred. Neither our precautions nor our warnings could stop their looting, though we did all we could . .

I had posted Spaniards in every street, so that when the people began to come out [to surrender]

they might prevent our allies from killing those wretched people, whose number was uncountable. I also told the captains of our allies that on no account should any of those people be slain; but there were so many that we could not prevent more than fifteen thousand being killed and sacrificed [by the Tlaxcalans] that day."

By August the resistance had been pushed into a single corner of Tlatelolco. The brigantines began moving into the canals, their gunners firing into the houses. Realizing the situation was hopeless, Cuauhtémoc loaded his family and retainers into canoes and attempted to escape to the mainland. The lake was covered with canoes as people fled the city. When Cortés realized what had happened he ordered the brigantines out into the lake to find the emperor. The crew of one ship recognized the imperial awnings, overtook the canoe, and forced it to surrender. Taken before Cortés, Cuauhtémoc said, "Lord Malinche, I have kept my obligation in the defense of my city and vassals, and I can do no more, and I am brought by force and impressment into your presence and power. Take that dagger in your belt and kill me."

Cortés responded graciously, praising the beleaguered emperor for his valiant defense. Although he regretted the destruction of the city and the deaths of so many people, he said it was now passed and could not be

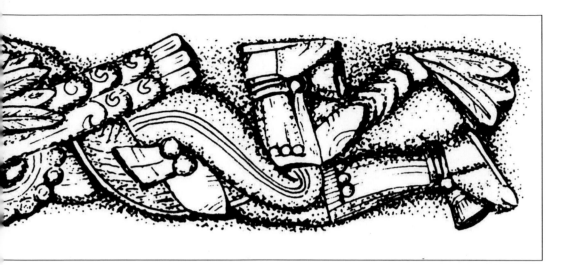

changed. As for Cuauhtémoc and his followers, their lives would be spared.

The great siege was over. With the Conquest of Mexico, one age in the history of the world ended, and a new one was beginning. In the simple, but soaring words of Bernal Díaz del Castillo, "Cuauhtémoc and his captains were apprehended on the thirteenth of August, at the hour of vespers, on the day

Cuauhtémoc, the last Aztec emperor of Mexico, on a 20th-century Mexican five peso coin. (Author's collection)

of the Honorable St. Hipolite, in the year of one thousand five hundred twenty-one. Thanks to Our Lord Jesus Christ, and to Our Lady, the Holy Virgin Mary, His blessed mother. Amen."

Bernal Díaz del Castillo, chronicler of the Conquest

"Bernal Díaz del Castillo, citizen and magistrate of the most loyal city of Santiago de Guatemala, one of the first discoverers and conquerors of New Spain and its provinces ..."

With these words, written some 30 years after the Conquest, a crusty, vain, honest old veteran began one of the greatest war memoirs of all time. Bernal Díaz del Castillo's *True History of the Conquest of New Spain* is just that – a true history. Whatever flaws or slips of memory it might contain (and there are remarkably few), it is not only one of the most accurate accounts of the Conquest, but also of the Aztec Empire at the height of its glory. No subsequent work on the Conquest or on Aztec Mexico can be written without it.

Like most Spaniards in Cortés's original band, Díaz was a Castilian, born in Medina

del Campo. The records of his early life are sketchy. The date of his birth is given as either 1492 or 1496. By his own account, he was the son of Francisco Díaz del Castillo, called "*El galán*" (the gallant or the handsome), a regidor or magistrate, and member of a quasi-noble class of squires known as *hidalgos*, or "people of substance." This position, while not one of great wealth, at least allowed Bernal an above-average education that is reflected in the *True History*.

There are no authentic portraits, but Díaz claimed to have been nicknamed *El galán* like his father, and in his own case he most certainly meant "the handsome." He was said to have been a *bon vivant* who tended to live beyond his means, an excellent conversationalist, and highly opinionated. He was an opportunist, open to any new ideas by which he might benefit, and touchy on what he felt was his just due. He was also a linguist. While in Cuba he learned the local language, appears to have picked up a basic proficiency in Nahuatl in Mexico, and, after eventually settling in Guatemala, spoke the Cakchiquel language of his Indian retainers there.

Díaz's story was typical of most of the soldiers who joined Cortés, having first tried their luck elsewhere in the New World. He left Spain in 1514 as part of the entourage of Pedro Arias de Ávila, who was sent to rule over the newly conquered province of Darien (now known as Panama). Disputes broke out between the brutal, iron-fisted Arias and his son-in-law, Vasco Núñez de Balboa, resulting in Balboa's execution. That, together with illness and a series of revolts against Arias's rule, left Díaz disillusioned,

Carved stone head of an Eagle knight, showing the determination of the warriors who faced Cortés. (Museo Nacional de Antropologia, Mexico)

and he departed for the recently conquered island of Cuba, where the governor, Diego Velásquez was his distant cousin.

By 1517, Díaz had spent three years in Panama and Cuba without accomplishing anything of importance. Determined to do better, he joined a group of Spaniards in the same situation, and together they took out loans and joined the expedition under Francisco Hernández de Córdoba. This first exposure to the North American mainland, while disappointing, convinced him that it held opportunities, and he subsequently joined Juan de Grijalva's expedition. By 1519, when the Cortés expedition was organizing, he was as close to being a seasoned expert on the Mexican coast as was possible in that era.

Díaz was a romantic, and can perhaps be forgiven for allowing a certain amount of romanticism to work its way into his reminiscences. He had, after all, known a world that no European had imagined, and that few would ever see. He was also influenced by *Amadís de Gaula*, a romantic novel written in medieval times and printed for the first time in 1508. It quickly became the most popular printed book in Spain, and most members of the Cortés expedition who were literate had read it. Díaz certainly had, because he compares the approach to the city of Mexico with "the enchantments that are told in the book of Amadís." Amadís also worked its way into his impressions of doña Marina because, writing in old age, he inadvertently drew parallels between her life and that of the fictional hero.

Like many soldiers of his era, he was both devout and worldly. He praised God for any outstanding turn of events in the Conquest. In battle, he believed that Christ had taken a personal interest in his survival, because otherwise he might not have lived to tell the tale. Yet for all his religious devotion, he was not above avarice and lust. Posted to guard Moctezuma, he asked a page to beg that Moctezuma "give me a beautiful Indian woman." Moctezuma summoned him, and said, "Bernal Díaz del Castillo, it has come to me that you have substantial garments and

gold, and I will order that you be given today a fine lady-in-waiting; treat her well, for she is the daughter of a lord; and I will also give you gold and mantles." To that, Díaz knelt, kissed his hands, and asked God's protection over him. When this was translated, Moctezuma purportedly remarked, "It seems to me that Bernal Díaz is a noble man."

Díaz's writings convey an unabashed respect for Moctezuma. Whenever he encountered the emperor, he always respectfully removed his helmet. For his part, Moctezuma was impressed to learn that Díaz had served on the Córdoba and Grijalva expeditions, of which he was well aware. The one point of contention was the matter of sacrifices which Moctezuma was required to offer as high priest of the state religion. Cortés attempted to dissuade him, and when the emperor promised not to kill human beings, agreed to allow him to go to the temple. A detachment of four captains, 150 soldiers, and one of the chaplains, Father de la Merced, accompanied him. Despite his promises, Moctezuma killed several men and boys, and Díaz and the other guards could only turn away and pretend they had not seen it. On returning to their quarters, however, their feelings were assuaged rather easily by Moctezuma's gift of gold jewelry.

The surrender of the city brought disappointment. Much of the treasure had disappeared, lost in the fighting that began on the *Noche Triste*. Discouraged, Díaz joined an expedition led by Gonzalo Sandoval that ventured south into the Valley of Oaxaca, then across the Isthmus of Tehuantepec to Coatzacoalcos on the Gulf of Mexico, where Díaz was given three land grants with large numbers of Indian tributaries.

In 1524 Cortés decreed that all married soldiers had 18 months to bring their wives to the country, and bachelors must marry, or forfeit their property. Díaz appears to have complied by entering into a common-law arrangement with an Indian woman with whom he was living at the time. Always restless, however, he joined Cortés's ill-fated expedition to Honduras that same year (see page 80), and in 1526, accompanied Pedro de Alvarado into Guatemala, passing through the region of the present city of Antigua, where ultimately he would make his home. Perhaps the thought already crossed his mind for, despite the fact that he was only in his late 20s or early 30s, illness and years of battle had left him feeling old and tired. Additionally, in the 1530s the king-emperor sent a cadre of bureaucrats to administer the new domains to the benefit of the Crown. Soldiers like Díaz, who had won the empire by their swords, lost their great landholdings at the stroke of a pen.

In 1539, armed with recommendations from Cortés and the viceroy, Antonio de Mendoza, Díaz went to Spain to defend his claims. Eventually he received compensation for the estates he had lost and confirmation of those he retained, and in 1541 he moved to Guatemala. There he received new estates and married Teresa Becerra de Durán, a well-to-do Spanish widow whose father, Bartolomé Becerra, had been one of the conquerors of Guatemala, and whose first husband, Juan Durán, was an early settler. Thus, he settled to the life of a wealthy planter, participating in local affairs, raising his children by Teresa, and securing legacies for those he had with various Indian mistresses.

Díaz was keenly aware that he had participated in events that changed the world, and that he himself had witnessed a civilization that was gone forever. In the preface to the *True History* he wrote: "That which I myself saw, and what I myself did in the fighting, as a good eye witness I will write, with the help of God, very simply, without twisting one part or another ... I am more than eighty-four years old and have lost my sight and hearing, and by my efforts I have no other wealth to leave to my children and descendants, other than this my true and wonderful story ..."

This appears to have been the final of three prefaces he drafted, for he was already at work on his manuscript in the early 1550s, when he would have been in his late 50s or early 60s. The work itself occupied the rest of his very long life. For all his pleas of poverty, Díaz was a prominent citizen of Guatemala, an extensive landholder, and member of the ruling council. His public duties and business interests occupied much of his time, and he put aside the memoir for months at a time. He even abandoned the manuscript for a while, following the publication of Francisco López de Gómara's *Crónica de la Nueva España* in 1552, feeling that López de Gómara had rendered his own work redundant. Díaz was angered, however, that López de Gómara gave all the credit to Cortés when he believed the success of the Conquest was due to the efforts of ordinary soldiers such as himself. He resumed his work, completed it, then continued rewriting and refining it until his death in his late 80s, at the beginning of 1584.

Whatever Díaz's indignation at López de Gómara's hagiography, the figure of Cortés dominates the *True History*. Díaz is aware of his deviousness and self-interest, yet there is no question that he admires him. Throughout the narrative, Diaz refers to him as "Our Cortés" or "Our Captain," and was obviously prepared to follow him anywhere.

Despite its antiquity, *True History* is timeless. It is an old soldier's reminiscences, devoid of any theories, political causes, or petitions for honor, and has a ring to it that would be recognized by soldiers of any era. Bernal Díaz del Castillo would find himself among comrades at any veterans' gathering of the 21st century.

Habsburg and Valois rivalry

A united Spain barely existed when Cortés embarked on the Conquest. At the dawn of the 16th century King Ferdinand ruled over an independent Aragón, while his wife, Isabella, reigned separately as queen of Castile. At the time of her death in 1504, they had two surviving children, Juana, who ascended to the Castilian throne, and Catherine who became the first of Henry VIII's six wives. The pathetic Queen Juana, known in Spanish history as *la loca* (the crazy), was mentally deranged, and the regency of Castile fell to her husband, Philip of Burgundy, son of the Holy Roman Emperor Maximilian I. Philip, however, died two years later, and Ferdinand assumed the regency. In the meantime, he had remarried, hoping to provide a male heir for Aragón. In this, he was no more successful than he had been with the first marriage, and with his death in 1516, both the Aragonese crown and the Castilian regency passed to Juana's eldest son, a 16-year-old-boy named Charles.

Charles was born in Flanders, where he had remained when his parents moved to Spain. Arriving with his Flemish entourage, in a country he had never seen, whose customs he did not understand, and whose various languages he could not speak, he insisted not simply upon being the regent for Castile, but to share its crown. Thus, the first king of a united Spain was a foreigner who inaugurated the Spanish branch of an Austrian dynasty, the Habsburgs.

The first Charles, accustomed to the wealth and splendor of Flanders, found in Spain, a country eking out a subsistence living, and a somber, austere court. Although this austerity bred the conquistadors, who ultimately would win him an empire beyond imagination, the sole imperial resources at this point were a few islands in the West Indies that brought virtually nothing compared to the great wealth Portugal gleaned from its African and East Indian trade. Even these possessions were of little interest to the new king. In early 1519, he learned that his grandfather Maximilian had died, initiating a scramble for the vacant imperial throne of the Holy Roman Empire (and by now essentially German). Among the chief contenders were his uncle by marriage, Henry VIII, and Francis I of France. Determined to win at all costs, Charles bribed the electors on an unprecedented scale and won the crown, although this created huge debts that Spain was expected to help absorb. Charles I of Spain was now Charles V of the Holy Roman Empire, and as such, he would be known to history. Henceforth there would be long periods of absentee rule while the king-emperor tended to his German holdings. For the next two centuries the interests of Spain would often be subordinated to the interests of the Habsburg family in central Europe. Spain, however, would shoulder the economic burden, frittering away much of the vast riches won by Cortés and others.

In the fall of 1519, Charles toured his Spanish dominions, which were now on the verge of rebellion. Grievances included the unanticipated debt, the consolidation of the monarchy, ignorance of Spanish customs and traditions by the king-emperor's Flemish appointees, and Charles's determination to depart for Germany the following year to accept the imperial crown. Amid this internal turmoil, Francisco de Montejo and Alonso Hernández de Puertocarrero arrived in Seville to press Hernán Cortés's case, bringing with them the first shipload of treasure from Mexico, and the delegation of Totonac Indians. Their ship and funds were impounded, and the treasure was deposited with the Casa de Contratación, the royal

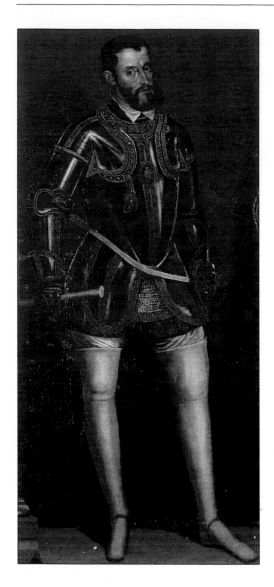

Charles V (1500–58) inherited his Spanish throne at the age of 16 and became Holy Roman Emperor in 1520. This enormous realm, with its numerous religious and political problems, was his primary focus of interest, but he was quick to see the advantages of investing in exploration in the New World. (Museo Nacional de Historia , Mexico)

Church's activities came at a time of growing nationalism in northern and central Europe. The German princes were tired of the meddling by an avaricious Italian papacy, and many people were demanding access to the Bible and liturgy in their own languages rather than Latin. The authority of the Roman Catholic Church, so long the bulwark of western European civilization, was being questioned for the first time.

Nevertheless, as Charles hurried through Spain travelling to the port of Corunna on the north coast and thence to Germany, he found time to invite Cortés's ambassadors Montejo and Puertocarrero to court. It took time to locate the king on his peregrinations, but when they did, they presented him with a petition calling for the recognition of the Cortés expedition as an official expedition of conquest, for release of its funds and ship, and for the supplies so urgently needed. On March 3, 1521, the treasures were displayed in court, and the Totonacs presented to the king and the *Cortes* the Castilian parliament.(The Spanish word *Cortes*, without the accented "e" means court; *Cortés* translates as "courteous"). Charles was particularly fascinated with the Indians, whom he ordered treated with extreme consideration.

Montejo and Puertocarrero were not the only representatives of the New World at court. En route back to Seville, they had stopped to reprovision in Cuba, where Diego Velásquez learned (probably through Montejo, who had divided loyalties) of the vast treasure on board the ship. The governor was furious. In April 1519, his deputy, Pánfilo de Narváez, had returned from Spain with a license for Velásquez himself to conquer Yucatán and what was dimly understood to be Mexico. Now, he learned that Cortés had beaten him to the

appraisal office that was responsible for the Indies, from whence Charles ordered it turned over to the keeper of the crown jewels.

Charles was anxious to leave Spain. Stung by the resentment of his Spanish subjects, he was even more concerned that his newly won suzerainty over Germany was crumbling. Two years earlier, a young professor of theology at the University of Wittenberg, Dr Martin Luther, had posted "Ninety-five Theses Upon Indulgences," calling for debate on the ecclesiastical practice of offering remittance from Divine punishment in exchange for a financial contribution. His public questioning of the

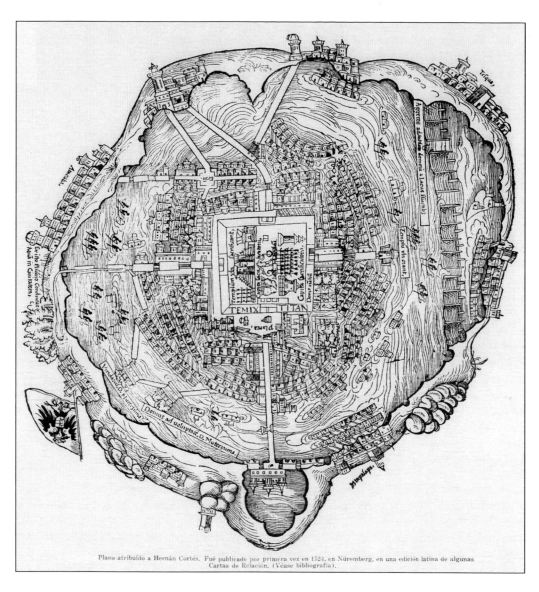

Plano atribuído a Hernán Cortés. Fué publicado por primera vez en 1524, en Nüremberg, en una edición latina de algunas Cartas de Relación. (Véase bibliografía).

Albrecht Dürer's plan of the City of Tenochtitlan/Mexico, attributed to Cortés, and first published in Nuremberg in 1524. This is an example of how European curiosity regarding the events in the New World spread across Europe, especially the Habsburg dominions of Charles V. (American Museum of Natural History)

punch, as it were. Aside from dispatching Narváez on his ill-fated mission to end the Cortés expedition, he held hearings, assembled evidence, and dispatched deputies to Spain to present his case.

Velásquez's representatives countered Montejo and Puertocarrero arguing that, far from being a loyal subject, Cortés was little more than a pirate and traitor. It was a wasted effort. Swayed, no doubt, by the treasure, the *Cortes* agreed to postpone any final decision between the two until both could be heard (and, no doubt, to wait and see whether Cortés succeeded or failed). The councilors even went so far as to suggest that Velásquez might do better by bringing a civil suit. Even more important, the ship was released, along with the money from Mexico for use as the Cortés adherents saw fit, specifically to purchase the necessary supplies. A few days later, the king departed for Germany. The Totonacs, who were beginning to suffer from the climate of northern Spain, were sent back to Seville. One died and the others ultimately were sent back to the Americas, although it appears they got no further than Cuba.

The Cortés expedition was not the only overseas venture on the king's mind. He had been persuaded to sponsor an expedition under Ferdinand Magellan, a Portuguese in Spanish service, which departed Spain in 1519 with five ships in an effort to fulfill Columbus's vision of reaching the East Indies by sailing west. Magellan discovered a passage around South America, sailed across the Pacific, arriving in the Philippines in 1521. Here he was killed in a fight with the natives, and the voyage continued by his lieutenant, Juan Sebastián del Cano, who arrived back in Spain with one ship and 18 men in September 1522. Although del Cano was awarded a coat of arms and a pension for becoming the first man to sail around the world, Charles V barely recovered his costs, further dampening his already marginal interest in exploration and conquest.

In fact, Charles's main goal was not overseas expansion, but to gain supremacy throughout Europe and lead a great crusade that would crush the Ottoman Turks, who now controlled much of the eastern Mediterranean. Luther and the Reformers were not the only threat to his dream. His chief rival was Francis I of France. Like Charles, Francis was young – barely out of his teens – and the first of a new dynasty. But where Charles's interest in Spain and the Indies was secondary compared to his concern over Germany, Francis was entirely devoted to French aggrandizement. He aspired to control the rich mercantile region of northern Italy, splitting Charles's domains in half, and making France the dominant power in Europe.

Physically no two men could have been more dissimilar. Charles was short and pale. No portrait, however flattering, could conceal the long jaw and protruding lower lip that came to define the Habsburgs. Even in languages he knew, his speech was so slow as to be almost incoherent, and some,

remembering his mother, questioned his mental capabilities, although his Burgundian heritage made him more urbane and sophisticated than his Spanish subjects. In short, he was a far cry from the rugged warrior kings that had dominated Castilian history and that Spaniards almost demanded.

Francis, on the other hand, was an outdoorsman, a skilled hunter, an excellent rider, and an accomplished wrestler. Well developed mentally as well as physically, he was the epitome of style and sophistication in a country that increasingly viewed itself as the center of cultural patronage and refinement. What France might lack, Francis provided by importing artistic geniuses like Leonardo da Vinci and Benvenuto Cellini. His portraits, the most famous of which is the oversized masterpiece by Jean Clouet now hanging in the Louvre, show a handsome, shrewd, self-confident man with a trace of smugness. Titian would paint both Francis and Charles in their later years: Francis is elegantly dressed in velvet, a worldly and totally commanding figure, while Charles appears grim and careworn, his face surrounded by armor. His cares began early. By 1521 when he finally declared Martin Luther an outlaw, the question had become academic. Already, many of the German princes had rallied around Luther, and Francis had allied himself with the Ottoman Empire in a war against Charles's domains.

Even in the Indies, there was no peace. Following Columbus's first voyage, the papacy had brokered a series of treaties aimed at quelling the rivalry between the Spaniards and Portuguese as to who should control the Indies trade. By the Treaty of Tordesillas in 1494 Portugal was given dominion over all territory east of the treaty line (sited some 370 miles west of the Azores), and the Spaniards received everything to the west. The overseas commerce of other nations, such as England and France, was negligible, and the possibility that they might involve themselves never occurred to anyone. With the accession of Francis to the French throne, however, this changed. Resenting Spain's claim to

Francis I (1494–1547), King of France and the chief rival to Spanish pretensions of supremacy in Europe. Francis also regarded the nascent Spanish empire in the Americas with interest and some jealousy, licensing the earliest of what became a long tradition of privateer attacks on the Spanish "treasure fleets" sailing back to Spain from the Caribbean. (Heritage Images Partnership)

monopoly in the New World, he was determined to get his share.

In 1523, with Mexico firmly in Spanish hands, a fleet departed for Seville loaded with treasure, New World produce, and exotic animals, the first major payoff of the Conquest. Approaching Cape St. Vincent, the ships were waylaid by French corsairs who seized almost 700 lb of pearls, 500 lb of gold dust, and cases of gold and silver ingots. The French had sailed under royal patronage, and Francis received ample share of the plunder. Henceforth, the French not only waylaid homebound Spanish ships (the so-called "Treasure Fleets"), but also began cruising the Indies, attacking commerce, and

trading with settlers in violation of Spain's royal monopoly. When Charles complained to the pope, Francis countered, "The sun shines for me as for the Spaniard."

It seemed that Charles could never escape the changes that the New World unleashed on his own inflexible world. Columbus's discoveries had brought into question thousands of years of accumulated knowledge. Not only had he found an unknown continent, but that continent contained people. Columbus, envisioning himself as Christopher, the Bearer of Christ, had expected to encounter Asians, recognized as humans with immortal souls and therefore candidates for salvation. The Indians of the New World, however, had been isolated for millennia from the mainstream of world affairs. They had developed entirely differently, and were unlike anyone known by the people of the Old World; regardless of nation, tribe, or culture, they were unique. This raised the question of whether they were even human, or instead some highly developed species of animal, capable of profound mimicry, architecture, and manual skill. For the early explorers and settlers of the West Indies, the question was hardly worth consideration. Assuming they were human (which many Europeans were unwilling to concede), some conquistadors regarded them as a subspecies, incapable of civilization or salvation. Therefore, in the view of the settlers, they were open to exploitation and abuse.

Yet there were those who insisted the Indians were children of God and must be treated as such. Among the most militant of these was Bartolomé de las Casas. Las Casas had come to the Indies in 1502, the classic adventurer-speculator, acquiring mines and estates where he relentlessly worked his Indian slaves. He was an enthusiastic participant in the vicious conquest of Cuba, and was rewarded with more estates and slaves. In about 1512 he took religious orders, but even then retained his estates and remained indifferent to the Indians. In 1514, however, the 40-year-old las Casas experienced a profound revelation concerning the atrocities he and his countrymen were inflicting on the Indians, and he devoted the remainder of his 92 years to being their champion.

Returning to Spain, las Casas met with Charles V, who, persuaded by his arguments, authorized the establishment of Indian utopian communities on the Venezuelan coast. This plan failed and las Casas retreated to Santo Domingo, where he began work on a vast treatise, part history, part prophecy, and part fabrication. Entitled *Brevísimia relación de la destrucción de las Indias* (A Very Brief Account of the Destruction of the Indies), it saw wide circulation throughout Europe. Translated (with embellishments) into English and Dutch, it formed the basis of the infamous "Black Legend" of Spanish atrocities that haunts relations between the English-speaking and Spanish-speaking worlds to this day.

On trips to Spain over the ensuing years, las Casas would continue to advise Charles. His discussion with the king-emperor got an additional boost in 1537, when Pope Paul III issued the bull *Sublimis Deus*, which proclaimed Indians to be children of God worthy of salvation. Charles's contribution was a legal code known as the New Laws that regulated conquest and colonization, tempered subjugation with salvation, and attempted to end exploitation by, among other things the abolition of the encomiendas, an effort that was only partially successful. Nevertheless, las Casas is still respected throughout Central America, and is one of the very few Spaniards honored in Mexico, as the "Apostle of the Indies."

Doña Marina

By the very nature of the Conquest, virtually everyone whose name is known to history was, in some form or another, a combatant. If there was a civilian, then it is one of the most important but least understood figures of those events – the mysterious Indian girl known to history as doña Marina. Although her existence and her pivotal role are well documented, details of her life are sparse, conflicting, and shrouded in legend. The Mexican view of her is schizophrenic. On the one hand, she is *La Malinche*, a female Quisling or Benedict Arnold who betrayed her people. Yet as the mother of Cortés's son Martín, the first recorded *mestizo* or mixed-blood that makes up the bulk of the modern Mexican population, she is the mother of the nation. This ambiguity, no doubt, stems to a large degree from her importance. In assuming her decisive position, willingly or otherwise, she went against the established norm of female nonentity expected in both Castilian and Aztec society, a status that combined and carried over into the traditional Mexican view of women.

Even her origins are shrouded in contradiction. At the time she was acquired by the Castilians she was perhaps 17, but possibly younger. It is almost certain her name was Malinalli, Hispanicized to Marina. Bernal Díaz invariably appended "doña" as a title of respect, possibly for her position as interpreter, or possibly for her position as Cortés's mistress, or both. He called her a "great chieftainess and daughter of great chieftains and mistress over vassals, and one could see this by her carriage." He added that when the women of Potonchán were distributed, Cortés initially gave her to Alonso Hernández de Puertocarrero, an old friend from his hometown of Medellín who also happened to be a cousin to the Count of Medellín. When Puertocarrero returned to Spain to press Cortés's case, Marina remained. Undoubtedly it would have been embarrassing for Puertocarrero in Spain with a mistress whose very humanity was not yet established in the Spanish mind. Likewise, it was essential for her to remain in Mexico as interpreter.

Most of the information concerning doña Marina comes from Bernal Díaz, who was the only contemporary writer to give a woman a significant role in the great events of the age. Certainly, Cortés, Alonso de Aguilar, and others mention her, but in Díaz's *True History*, she holds an honored position almost equal to Cortés himself. Díaz, who was not writing with the hope of any serious personal gain, appears to have recognized (or at least admitted) more than the others that without doña Marina, there would have been no Conquest. His account of her life is that generally accepted in Mexico.

So far so good. But as Díaz's writing progressed, he unwittingly helped create a legend surrounding her origin. Evidence indicates she was born in what is now the State of Tabasco, on the southeastern marches of the Aztec Empire, either in 1502 or 1505. Her birth occurred on the day of Malinal, in the 12th month of the Mexican year, and for that reason she was named Malinalli. The accepted version of her life, based largely on Díaz, indicates her father was lord of the village of Painala, about 25 miles from Coatzacoalcos, and her mother, the ruler of the nearby village of Xaltipán. After her father's death, her mother married another local ruler and produced a son, whom the parents wanted to inherit all three fiefdoms, including that of Marina's father which was rightfully hers. Consequently, Marina was sold to traveling merchants, and sold again, until she ended up in Potonchán.

Atlivetzyan.

Cortés makes peace with the Tlaxcalans. The artist probably saw doña Marina, and the likenesses in the *Lienzo* are as good as any. From the *Lienzo de Tlaxcala*, Plate 4. (American Museum of Natural History)

Francisco López de Gómara, who drew his information from Cortés, tells essentially the same story, differing only in detail. In his version, Marina's parents were wealthy – but not necessarily noble – citizens in the village of Viluta (correctly rendered Olutla), likewise near Coatzacoalcos. Rather than being sold to merchants, Marina was kidnapped by them. The result is the same: eventual arrival in Potonchán, where she encounters the Castilians. In his account, she is less a working partner to Cortés than a loyal servant and concubine.

Now, however, the parallels end, as Díaz begins to blend her story in with other, more familiar tales. He tells of a reconciliation

with her parents, strongly reminiscent of a similar reconciliation of the fictional hero Amadís. In both cases, their conversion to Christianity prompts them to forgive those who have wronged them, explaining that their misfortunes ultimately led to their conversions to the True Faith. It also brings to mind the biblical story of Joseph, betrayed and sold by his blood kin, only to rise to power among the alien people of Egypt.

López de Gómara downplayed doña Marina's role as much as Díaz played it up, and of the two, Díaz is the more believable. Her true role was probably somewhere between that of servant-concubine and conquistadora. It is doubtful that Cortés would have accomplished so much – if indeed he could have accomplished anything at all – without her help. As much as a feat of arms, the Conquest of Mexico was a triumph of diplomacy, in recognizing and exploiting the divisions and hatreds between the various Indian states. Doña Marina was essential to the Spaniards' understanding of all the implications of local rivalries. Given the strong, almost inseparable bond that existed between Marina and Cortés during the Conquest, there can be little doubt that Marina's loyalty was based on love and admiration as much as servitude. For his part, Cortés seemed to view women in general as a means of pleasure or policy, but if he was capable of love, his attention toward Marina is some indication.

Cortés on campaign, however, was not the same as Cortés projecting his image to the Spanish court and to posterity. Barring the possibility of some mention in his now lost First Letter, Marina appears only twice in his correspondence, once in the Second Letter, in which he referred to her as "my interpreter, who is an Indian woman from Putunchan," and in the Fifth, written from Honduras more than four years later, where he called her "Marina, who traveled always in my company after she had been given me as a present with twenty other women." Through the pen of López de Gómara, Cortés acknowledged his illegitimate children by Marina and others, and López de Gómara allowed himself a veiled disapproval of his patron's relationships with the native women. Nevertheless, the relationship itself is carefully skirted. Whatever Cortés might have felt for Marina, he could not expect to present himself at court as the harbinger of civilization and champion of Christianity while having an intense and history-making affair with an Indian girl.

Yet, reading between the lines, there is no question that he depended on her. The Second Letter describes how "the Indian woman" uncovered the massacre plot in Cholula. The Fifth Letter tells of how she recited the deeds of the Castilians to Honduran chiefs, reinforcing stories they had already heard from the Tabascan Indians. The Mexicans themselves thoroughly understood her role. The name by which they called Cortés, *Malinche* (probably *Malintzin*, transliterated by Díaz and Aguilar as *Malinche*) signified his role as "Marina's Captain" or "Marina's Lord," although in modern Mexico the term is applied to doña Marina herself.

In 1522, Marina gave birth to Martín Cortés, the conqueror's eldest son. Two years later, during the expedition to Honduras, Cortés married her off to Juan Jaramillo, by whom she had a daughter. She also received estates in Tabasco, where she apparently spent most of her time until her death in 1551. According to the 19th-century historian William Hickling Prescott, Martín became a prominent citizen of New Spain, and knight companion of the Order of Santiago. In 1568, however, he and his legitimate half-brother, also named Martín were suspected of treason, and tortured. They remained incarcerated until 1574.

The Conquest was the great event of doña Marina's life. Aside from the scant information about her estates and her marriage to Jaramillo, she gradually faded from history. Even so, her essential role in Cortés's success cannot be disputed. Prescott, a product of New England Puritanism with all its prejudices towards women as the "weaker vessel," and whose account of the Conquest is as much literature as history, nevertheless paid her homage when he wrote: "That remarkable woman had attracted general admiration by the constancy and cheerfulness with which she endured all the privations of the camp. Far from betraying the weakness and timidity of her sex, she had shrunk from no hardship herself, and had done much to fortify the drooping spirits of the soldiers; while her sympathies, whenever occasion offered, had been actively exerted in mitigating the calamities of her Indian countrymen."

Prescott did not exaggerate. For three years, this teenager who changed history was the most important woman in the world.

Rebuilding and rebellion

Once the Castilians had conquered the Mexican capital, their immediate thoughts were centered on spoils of war. For three years they had fought and suffered against incredible odds. They had seen their comrades dragged to the temples for sacrifice, and had been powerless to intervene. They had recovered identifiable body parts which had been offered to the pagan gods. Now it was time for payment. The day of the surrender, they raged through the city looking for gold. Meanwhile, their Tlaxcalan allies continued their hideous orgy of blood, slaughtering any Mexican they found. The city itself was completely ruined. About 100,000 men, women, and children had died during the 80-day siege, and thousands of corpses lay unburied. Most of the remaining population streamed out along the causeways where the Spaniards set up checkpoints to search for concealed treasure. Noblewomen covered themselves with mud and dressed in rags to hide their status, but the rapacious Castilians subjected them all to body searches.

Once a substantial amount of gold was collected, it was taken to Cortés's headquarters in Coyoacán, where he and the Crown auditors agreed to have it melted down and assayed. The total came to more than 130,000 *castellanos*.[3] This and all other plunder, including slaves, was tabulated. One-fifth of the total was allocated to the Crown in accordance with the law. The balance was distributed to the army according to rank, with Cortés and his captains naturally getting the lion's share. Additionally, there was a substantial amount of gold ornaments, featherwork, and other objects that the sophisticated Cortés recognized as art. Rather than being parceled out as plunder, these were sent *in toto* to the less than appreciative king-emperor, who had the gold melted down. Much of the featherwork eventually ended up in Vienna, where, if one searches diligently enough, one may see it in the Künsthistorische Museum.

The amount of plunder proved disappointing. The great treasure found in the palace and then lost on the *Noche Triste* was gone. As previously noted, the men had served on their own account, and now that the war was over, their accumulated debts had to be paid. Some were so substantial that arbitrators were called in to determine just amounts, and those without the money to pay were given a two-year grace period. With the constant fear and stress of the war behind them, the soldiers began to consider their positions and, for the first time, began to mutter against their commander, believing he had amassed a great personal fortune at their expense. The royal auditors, likewise, accused him of withholding treasure that rightfully belonged to the Crown. They little realized that they were dealing not only with the losses of war, but with the highly developed private enterprise system of Aztec Mexico; much of the wealth they had seen throughout the city on their arrival two years earlier belonged not to the state, but to the city's powerful merchant class. These merchants, naturally, had fled with all they could carry.

His back to the wall, Cortés summoned Cuauhtémoc and the other lords to explain the loss. They argued among themselves, but could add little. The royal auditor, Julián Aldrete, demanded that Cuauhtémoc and Tetlepanquetzal, the king of Tacuba, be tortured. Cortés assented, probably with fewer qualms than he later pretended.

---

3 A *castellano* was 42.29 g of pure silver. There were 450 copper *maravedis* to the peso and 485 *maravedis* to the *castellano*.

Their feet were dipped in oil and set ablaze. Finally, Cuauhtémoc said the treasure had been thrown into the lake, but Castilian divers found little that was substantial. Ultimately, this brutality, which left both men permanently lamed, yielded only an additional 200,000 pesos. Once the Crown, the royal bureaucrats, Cortés, and the captains got their shares, the average soldier may have had about 160 pesos for three years of suffering. To put this in perspective, a reasonable sword cost about 50 pesos at the time.

Although large regions of Mesoamerica remained to be subdued, the Conquest was essentially completed with the surrender of Cuauhtémoc. The destruction of the greatest power on the continent had a profound effect on the surrounding states. The only other power capable of serious and prolonged opposition was the Tarascan empire, to the northwest in Michoacán. When word of the Mexican surrender reached the Tarascans, they sent emissaries to Cortés asking to be accepted as vassals. "I replied that we were, in truth, all Your Majesty's vassals," he reported to Charles V, "and that their lord had been wise in wishing to become one also, for we were obliged to make war on those who did not."

Nevertheless, he sent several expeditions to Michoacán, culminating with a reasonably large force (considering the resources) under Cristóbal de Olíd in the summer of 1522. As an example, Olíd plundered the region, throwing down the temples, and sent the Tarascan monarch to Mexico. There, Cortés received him with the full dignity of a ruler, and he returned to Michoacán duly impressed and subdued. Olíd, meanwhile, moved farther north to Colima, which he quickly pacified. Elsewhere, expeditions reached the Pacific. Cortés himself led an expedition to subdue the Pánuco region, in order to head off another colonization attempt by Governor Garay. In one of the towns, they found the flayed facial skin of Castilians from Garay's first expedition. Nevertheless, the Pánuco was subjugated, adding a great agricultural region to the growing empire.

The most remarkable aspect of these expeditions was the number of native auxiliaries under their own chieftains and lords, many of whom had recently been enemies. Besides Tlaxcalans, they included Texcocans, and even some 15,000 Mexicans provided by Cuauhtémoc and commanded by one of his cousins. The reason for the turnabout was really quite simple: their religion had long foretold the destruction of their world, and now it had come to pass. There was nothing further to do but to assist those who had overthrown that world. Thus, with the help of the defeated Aztecs, virtually all of what is now Mexico came firmly under Spanish rule within a decade or so. Such resistance as did occur came largely from some Maya-controlled areas of Yucatán, which managed to hold out for another century, and in some coastal and desert areas of the far north, to which the Spaniards did not attach any immediate importance. As Cortés noted in his third letter to Charles V, written only nine months after Cuauhtémoc's surrender, "Your Majesty's farms and estates have been established in the cities and provinces which seem the best and most suitable."

Interestingly enough, Cortés also worried about the fate of the Indians. Although he was the instrument of its destruction, he admired much of their civilization, and believed them capable of going about their business unmolested by their new rulers. He was growing particularly uneasy at the thought of enslaving them. Discussing the problem in one of his letters to the emperor, he contended they were of too high a caliber to be relegated to slavery and oppressed to destruction, as was happening in the West Indies. Realistically, however, if they were not enslaved, who would work the estates that the conquistadors were establishing? Additionally, entire regions had served as allies during the war and, far from being enslaved, their leaders expected to share in the spoils. To avoid outright slavery, yet maintain the economy, he recommended the establishment of an *encomienda*, a system already existing in the West Indies, by which

The grim visage of Xipe Totec, the flayed god of spring and the harvest, grins through a mask of his own skin in a small clay representation from Tlatelolco. Those sacrificed to Xipe Totec were flayed, and their skins worn as ceremonial costumes by the priests. Almost every god and goddess in the Mexican pantheon demanded human lives as sacrifice, the difference being only in the detail of the death. (Author's collection)

a conquistador or settler would be granted a fixed amount of labor from the Indians living on a specified area of land. The *encomendero* as the grantee was called, was expected to serve as a guardian of the Indians, to Christianize them, and have them ready for military service if called upon. Cortés required that every *encomendero* plant agricultural produce, which led to the introduction of European food crops into New Spain.

In practice it was much easier for the *encomendero* to require the payment of produce comparable to the specified labor, rather than to go out and attempt to keep a tally on who was working where and when. Consequently the system developed into a tribute, not radically different from that maintained by the Aztecs before the Conquest. With the *encomendero* essentially assuming the role previously held by the native princes, it required little serious adjustment. Although technically the *encomienda* was abolished under the New

Laws and other royal edicts, in reality it remained in one form or another, establishing a serfdom that lasted well into the 19th century; some contend that in parts of Mexico it continues.

As more of the country fell to the Castilians, Cortés realized it needed an administrative center. Although the ruined and pestilential city of Mexico had been abandoned after the surrender, he realized the psychological hold it had over the country. Perhaps, also, he did not want the ruins to become a place of pilgrimage for the defeated peoples, and a possible inspiration for rebellion. In late 1521, he decided to rebuild the city. Town lots were distributed to all who wanted them, and the city was divided into districts governed by various officials according to Spanish custom. While the reconstruction took place, the future population continued to reside in Coyoacán. Nevertheless, by May 1522, he was able to write to the king, "In the four or five months that we have been rebuilding the city it is already most beautiful ... each day it grows more noble, so that just as before it was the capital and center of all these provinces so it shall be henceforth. And it is being so built that the Spaniards will be strong and secure and well in charge of the natives, who will be unable to harm them in any way."

Initially, the job of rebuilding fell to Alvarado. The native auxiliaries, now more a hindrance than an asset, were given ample share of the plunder, and their leaders reconfirmed as lords of the provinces under the new order. Those not necessary to cleaning and rebuilding the city were sent home. Alvarado's tenure as supervisor of reconstruction was shortlived. Early in 1522 he was given the task of subduing Oaxaca, where he remained over a year, collecting substantial treasure. He was en route back to Mexico when he received word from Cortés that the treasure was to be forwarded on to the capital to replace that captured by the French corsairs of Francis I. Alvarado's men, who had imagined themselves wealthy from the plunder, were outraged, and several hatched a plot to murder him and his brothers. Getting wind of it, he arrested the plotters. Two ringleaders were hanged, and the local chief, also part of the conspiracy, was imprisoned, where he died two weeks later. This plot was an early indication of the growing discontent that would plague Cortés and his captains as the Conquest drew to a close.

New Spain and new legacies

If Balboa's expedition to Panama was the first European toehold on the mainland of the western hemisphere, the Conquest of Mexico was the first squeeze of a vise-like grip that kept more than half of the New World in Spanish hands for some three centuries. As with Columbus before him, the full import of Cortés's achievement was not understood for several decades. Yet Columbus, with his discovery of a continent previously unknown in Europe, and Cortés, with the conquest of a powerful and equally unknown empire, had proven that the unimaginable was possible. They set the stage for expeditions of Francisco Pizarro and others in South America, and for Francisco Vásquez de Coronado and Hernando de Soto in what is now the United States. In view of the accomplishments of Columbus and Cortés, the search for El Dorado, or for seven golden cities made perfect sense.

Meanwhile, Mexico became the centerpiece of a vast viceregency designated "New Spain" that extended from the modern American states of Utah and California, south to the Costa Rica–Panama border, and from Puerto Rico in the east across half the world to the Philippines. The administrative seat was the city of Mexico, which rose like a phoenix from the ashes of the Aztec capital. New Spain was the first of a series of viceregencies that extended southward across the hemisphere as Spanish power itself expanded. Next came Peru, which administered western South America; New Granada, northern South America; and finally La Plata, southeastern South America. Only Brazil, firmly in the hands of Portugal, escaped Spanish rule.

It is questionable whether any man besides Cortés could have conquered Mexico. Some argue that if he had not, someone else would have. But as Hugh Thomas notes in his magnificent history of the Conquest, this is totally conjecture and cannot be established.

The questions must then be raised: would any European besides Cortés have grasped and exploited the differences between the various Indian people? Given the record of most of his contemporaries, who tended to regard all Indians as beneath contempt, it is highly unlikely, and these political and tribal differences were essential to a Castilian victory. Could any other leader have been so profoundly lucky, and then be blessed with the good sense to realize it? Could any other leader have kept such an absolute hold over an army that was largely composed of unruly adventurers? Not until the city of Mexico had actually fallen, and the Aztec Empire was relegated to history did Cortés's own men seriously question his leadership. One must particularly admire his ability to maintain the loyalty of his Indian allies in the critical period before the final advance, when the *Noche Triste* had demonstrated how truly vulnerable the Castilians were.

What would have happened had the Conquest failed? Again, Thomas makes a good case that possibly Spain would have had second thoughts before another attempt at conquest, and that Mexico, like Japan, might then have gone its own way, remaining culturally isolated only to reemerge into European consciousness in a later era.

This, however, is speculation. As Cortés worked with the real problems of consolidating the newly won empire and rebuilding its capital, an entirely new complication arose. His wife, doña Catalina, arrived uninvited and unexpected from Cuba, bringing with her a retinue suitable for her presumed position as the new vicereine. At the time, Cortés had several mistresses, Indian and Castilian, and was preparing for the birth of his son by doña Marina. The pair argued and that, combined with the 7,500-foot altitude of Mexico City, no doubt aggravated doña

Catalina's already weak heart. She died under mysterious circumstances, and he was accused of murdering her. Most likely, however, they argued, and this brought on a fatal heart attack.

Don Antonio de Mendoza (1490–1552), who became viceroy of New Spain in 1535, was the first of a long line of bureaucrats who replaced the original conquerors in administering the new domains. (Museo Nacional de Historia, Mexico)

Equally suspicious was the death of Francisco de Garay, who was brought back to Mexico after his failed second expedition to Pánuco. After dining with Cortés on Christmas Day, 1523, Garay died of an unspecified stomach complaint.

By now, the old restlessness was setting in. Cortés had dispatched Cristóbal de Olíd to Honduras, and in 1524 received word that Olíd had rebelled. Using this as a pretext (and unaware that Olíd had already been defeated and executed by Cortés's supporters), he set off with several thousand Spaniards and native auxiliaries, and all the retinue of a court; he even took in tow the nominal emperor Cuauhtémoc. The expedition was a fiasco, beset by starvation, disease, and rumors of mutiny. When it returned to Mexico two years later, there were less than 100 survivors. Cuauhtémoc was not among them; exhausted, paranoid, and suspecting the emperor was conspiring against him, Cortés ordered him hanged in what is now the state of Guerrero, in southern Mexico.

The remainder of Cortés's life was anticlimactic. He and all the others who had fought so hard, and with such high hopes of fame, wealth, and glory, found themselves displaced by paper-shuffling bureaucrats sent by Charles V to administer the newly conquered kingdom. The rest of Cortés's life was divided between his estates in Mexico and in presenting his case to the king-emperor. He was named Marqués del Valle de Oaxaca, confirmed as captain-general, and given large estates, but he was denied the right to rule his conquests. That would be left to the civil servants, and in the early years, Mexico was governed by some remarkably good ones. Nevertheless, whispering campaigns, prompted largely by envy, prevented Cortés from receiving his full due, and in the end he was treated shabbily. He died on December 2, 1547, bitter, broken, and forgotten. His body was later returned to Mexico City, where it was buried in the Hospital of Jesus, which he had founded at the height of his power and prestige.

The fiery Pedro de Alvarado used the Conquest as the stepping stone to his own career as explorer and conqueror. Subjugating Guatemala, he was appointed governor of that province and of Honduras, but, as restless as his old commander, he could not resist new adventures. In 1541 he was assisting the acting governor of Jalisco, Cristóbal de Oñate, in besieging a native town. He was on foot in full armor when a horse slipped and fell on him. Crushed under the weight of horse and armor, he died about an hour later. Even in death, he was not safe from the bureaucrats, and within a year, his widow had lost many of his estates to the Crown.

In the end, it might be argued that the ordinary soldiers, like crusty old Bernal Díaz reminiscing on his Guatemalan estates, gained the most. They, after all, had learned to expect the least. Díaz complained of poverty, but poverty is relative. Compared to what might have been, he was, indeed, poor. But by the standards of his era or ours, he ended his days a wealthy man.

The Conquest inaugurated a bitter history of foreign intervention in Mexico. After Spain came military invasions by the United States and France, followed by the economic colonialism of Great Britain, the Netherlands, Germany, and, once again, the United States. This has left Mexico with a particularly xenophobic nationalism. Although the average Mexican takes a kindly and gracious view of foreigners as individuals, he does not necessarily feel the same toward the nations of which they are citizens.

The uneasiness toward foreigners began toward the end of the colonial period, as the winds of the Enlightenment, and the full implications of U.S. independence from Great Britain drifted into Mexico, creating a sense of nationhood. Spain, by then in irreversible decline, could do little to maintain Mexican loyalty. In fact, there had been little during the entire colonial period to inspire allegiance. Although the people of the New World dominions were technically Spanish subjects, and the New World provinces themselves were designated as "kingdoms" rather than colonies, the relationship was one of master and serf, and a foreign master at that. Civil administration was in the hands of *Peninsulares*, people born in Spain, or European-born foreigners in Spanish service, for whom Mexico was little more than a career assignment. They were forbidden by law to own estates, livestock, or interest in mines in the areas of their jurisdiction. This law was designed to avoid corruption and conflicts of interest, but on those rare occasions when it was enforced, it only increased the sense of estrangement between ruler and subject.

Below the *Peninsulares* were the *Creoles*, Spaniards of pure European descent but born in the New World, who made up the landed gentry and the officer corps of the colonial armies, but by-and-large were prohibited from participating in civic affairs. The third class was the *Mestizo*, the mixed bloods, who were mainly small merchants, artisans, and craftsmen. At the bottom were the native Indians, whose sole purpose was to serve as laborers. Such a caste system effectively stifled any effort at advancement by Mexicans of whatever ancestry, and when the Spanish regime collapsed in 1821, the country was ill-prepared for self-government. The first decades of independence were largely a history of military dictatorships, as the *Creole* generals were the only ones with any sort of administrative experience.

Even independence did not completely remove Spain from the scene. For several years afterwards, the Spaniards continued to hold the fortress of San Juan de Ulúa, guarding the entrance to Veracruz, and in 1829 Spain actually made a futile attempt to reoccupy the country, which resulted in its final expulsion. As late as the 1840s, however, Mexican monarchists conspired with Spanish representatives to place a Spanish prince on the now defunct Mexican throne.

This long heritage of ill-feeling has produced a Mexican attitude toward Spain that is, at best, ambiguous. While other nations in Latin America honor the old discoverers and conquerors on coins, monuments, and with street names, and the like, there is scarcely a mention of Cortés,

who was among the least cruel in an age when cruelty reigned. Conversely, Cuauhtémoc is a national hero, and his name and presumed likeness appear everywhere. Perhaps the final expression of national indifference was Mexico's refusal to establish diplomatic relations with the Franco regime in Spain.

The chaos of Mexico in the mid-19th century produced one of those ironies that so delight historians. During the French intervention of 1862–67, Napoleon III convinced the Habsburg Archduke Maximilian to accept the Mexican throne. He reigned for three years, struggling against an opposition Republican government led by Benito Juárez, a full-blooded Zapotec Indian. When French support was withdrawn, the empire collapsed, and Maximilian surrendered to the Republicans. More than three centuries earlier, a Castilian adventurer had conquered Indian Mexico on behalf of a Habsburg prince. Now Juárez, the Mexican Indian, ordered the death of a Habsburg prince.

Regardless of how the Mexicans might feel, the Conquest did occur, and the Spanish imprint on Mexican life and culture is everywhere. Every Mexican city and town that existed prior to the 20th century has its colonial monuments. The churches copy those of Spain, many of which were influenced by or converted from the mosques of Spanish Islam. The houses of the well-to-do, plain and drab on the outside and luxurious inside, can likewise be traced to Muslim Spain. Aside from the Spanish Islamic influence, one also sees majestic Renaissance and Baroque colonial mansions and public buildings. The great city of Guanajuato, a cradle of Mexican independence, is nevertheless entirely European, a center of Castilian culture in the New World, with its modern statues of don Quixote de la Mancha and the faithful Sancho Panza, and an annual Cervantes festival.

Yet the Castilian influence goes beyond art, literature, and architecture. It permeates the daily lives of the Mexican people. They speak a Mexicanized form of Castilian which, in Mexico, is referred to simply as

"Spanish." They use Napoleonic law, and their social attitudes historically have reflected those of Spain.

Most remarkable, however, is the blending that has occurred. Over the centuries Mexicans have taken the best (and sometimes the worst) aspects of both cultures, to create a new one that fits their conjoined national personality. The most obvious sign is on the faces of the people themselves. Martín Cortés might have been the first Mexican of mixed blood, but the European-Indian mix now accounts for at least 70 percent of the nation. In the far north, around the states of Nuevo León and Coahuila, and in the Bajío region of west central Mexico, between the cities of Guanajuato and Morelia, European origins predominate. And only in the rural areas does one see people who are predominantly Indian. The rest of the country's uncountable millions show the physical heritage of both races. At times, the mixed ancestry appears in individual families, with some siblings pale and European, others dark reddish-brown with high cheeks, and yet others having the characteristics of both.

The Spanish desire for gold was equaled only by their zeal to impose their own religion. Interestingly enough, Christianity took root with remarkable ease. To the people, the destruction of the Aztec civilization meant their own gods had deserted them, creating a spiritual void. Additionally, the Mexican concept of gods shedding their own blood, and the blood offerings in their temples meant that little mental adjustment was required to accept the notion of a god-king offering His blood for the benefit of the world, or the symbolic "drinking of blood" in the Christian Communion. In fact, there were enough parallels that the distinction between native belief and Christianity became blurred, creating a uniquely Mexican form of Catholicism. Ancient rituals are celebrated on Christian holidays, and many of the old gods have been transposed onto Christian saints with similar characteristics. Perhaps the most famous is the Virgin of Guadalupe,

which tradition states appeared to a humble Indian, Juan Diego, at Tepeyac in 1531. Interestingly enough, Tepeyac was sacred to the goddess Tonantzin, who was also viewed as a sort of mother figure.

Ironically, the founders of this new faith were the earliest Spanish friars, who did not study the old beliefs, and therefore did not recognize the continuing practice of ancient ways under the guise of Christianity. The first missionary to realize this was the Franciscan Bernardino de Sahagún (1499–1590), who spent the latter two-thirds of his long life in Mexico, and was the first to apply what we now would call anthropological field work to studying virtually every aspect of pre-Conquest Mexico. Sahagún's monumental *Historia general de las cosas de la Nueva España* ("General History of the Things of New Spain"), more popularly known as the *Florentine Codex*, is a detailed study of virtually every aspect of pre-Conquest life in Mexico, from history, religion, and philosophy, to trade and economics.

There is no question that Sahagún's motivation was to understand Mexican beliefs so that he could combat idolatry. Yet as the work progressed, it almost took on a life of its own. Working through his Mexican students, who had supplemented their own Nahuatl language with Castilian and Latin, Sahagún met with native elders and scholars, studying their pictorial records, and listening to their accounts of their now vanished world. The linguistic aspect fascinated him. Although Nahuatl was devoid of a formal style of writing, the Mexicans nevertheless used pictographs to express an idea. Many of these were reproduced in the *General History* together with the Nahuatl record written in the Roman alphabet, and its Castilian paraphrase and commentary. Sahagún studied Aztec monuments, and found much to admire in their history and culture. The basic work, compiled from about 1558 to 1580, was organized, European style, into 12 books categorized according to subject, with the text divided into chapters and paragraphs. The 12th book, a history of the Conquest itself,

DN FER-   NAN-   -DO   COR-   TES EN LA CONQUIS-TA DE MEXICO   ESTE ESTANDAR-TE FUE EL QUE TRAJO

was expanded into a much more extensive account in 1585, based on subsequent research with allowances for changes in Sahagún's own perspectives. When completed, the *General History* was so comprehensive, and the main body so dispassionate, that it must serve as the basis of any modern work on the Aztec civilization.

Another important account of ancient Mexico originated with an equally unlikely source, the Spanish Crown. There exists today in the Bodleian Library in Oxford, an earlier manuscript than either Sahagún or Durán, known as the *Codex Mendoza*. It was compiled in Mexico City about 1541 by

The banner of the Conquest. Most of the conquistadors believed their survival was entirely due to the protection of Christ and the saints, and this ensured that their religious observances were regular and fervent. (Topham Picturepoint)

native scribes working under friars, at the instigation of Charles V, who wanted to know more about his overseas dominions. Because the imperial commission for the manuscript apparently came from the viceroy, don Antonio de Mendoza, it carries his name.

The text of the *Codex Mendoza* combines the Mexican glyphs with written explanations in Castilian and Nahuatl. As such, it serves, in

LEFT A detail from the *Florentine Codex*, showing Bernardino de Sahagún (1499–1590), the Spanish missionary who chronicled the languages, customs and habits of the peoples of the New World in minute detail. (American Museum of Natural History)

ABOVE The Atlantes Temple and colonnade was part of the ceremonial center of the Toltec capital at Tula, some 60 miles north of Mexico City. The Aztecs viewed themselves as heirs to the Toltecs, and used the lingering Toltec mystique to establish their own legitimacy. (Instituto Nacional de Antropologia e Historia, Mexico)

the words of one scholar, as "a kind of Rosetta stone." The glyphs and illustrations portray virtually every aspect of Mexican society, including tributary kingdoms, lists of tribute, illustrations of textiles, arms and armor, costumes, foods, and even the thread of daily life for citizens of various classes. As such, it is a comprehensive visual image of the Aztec empire.

The inspiration for much of this work came from Juan de Zumárraga, the first Bishop of Mexico, who initially arrived in the country in 1528. Like the early settler Bartolomé de las Casas, Zumárraga saw himself as a protector of the Indians. His methods, however, were far more subtle than those of las Casas. For that reason, plus the fact that he also served as apostolic inquisitor, history often pillories him as a guardian of the conquering status quo. Yet, despite his zeal in protecting and expanding the faith, Zumárraga promoted learning and was open to different ideas. He believed that the Mexicans were capable of acquiring the best of Castilian culture, and also that (religion aside) their own culture contained

much that was admirable. The schools that he founded or sponsored paved the way for the Nahua-Castilian scholars who were indispensable to men like Sahagún and Durán. It was Zumárraga, also, who purportedly interviewed Juan Diego concerning his vision of the Virgin of Guadalupe. Although the validity of the apparition, and even the actual existence of Juan Diego has been questioned by both

Roman Catholic and non-Roman Catholic scholars, Pope John Paul II nevertheless canonized Juan Diego as a saint of the Church during his Episcopal visit to Mexico in the fall of 2001.

The Atlantes Temple, was an important Toltec center, but was slightly overshadowed by its rivals Teotihuacán and Cholula. (©Philip Baird www.anthroarcheart.org)

A modern reconstruction shows the precinct of the Great Temple of Mexico as it appeared about 1519. The Temple itself, surmounted by the twin sanctuaries of Huitzilopochtli and Tlaloc is on the left. Immediately in front is the round platform for gladiatorial sacrifices, and the round temple of Quetzalcoatl. To the right is the Great *Tzompantli*, the rack displaying the heads of sacrificial victims, and immediately in front, the ball court. (Museo Nacional de Antropologia, Mexico)

Today, vestiges of Aztec might are everywhere. The modern city of Mexico, built directly on top of the Aztec capital, is a treasure house of the pre-Conquest. Virtually any public works project uncovers some aspect of the original city. The construction of the great metro system in the late 1960s and early 1970s, and even something so mundane as sewer line repairs, have led to important new discoveries. Before visiting these sites, one would do best to orient oneself by seeing the two great museums in Chapultepec. The modernistic National Museum of Anthropology chronicles Mexico's past prior to the Conquest. Across the great boulevard of the Reforma, the National Museum of History in the old viceregal residence at Chapultepec Castle, itself a witness to much of Mexico's past,

covers the nation since 1519. The Museum of Anthropology displays many examples of Aztec art including the most famous of all, the great Calendar Stone. But examining the statues, paintings, and dioramas, one cannot escape the all-pervading feeling of violence and death.

Chapultepec Castle crowns the hill that gives the structure and surrounding district their names (Chapultepec means "hill of the grasshoppers"). The hill rises from a cypress grove that was already ancient when the Aztec rulers used the area as a summer retreat and hunting park. At the base of the hill are the springs that provided water to the city, not only in Aztec times, but throughout the entire colonial period, and the remains of the baths of the Aztec overlords. The castle itself preserves relics of the Conquest, including one of the banners of Hernán Cortés, a replica of which was featured in the 1948 film *Captain From Castile*. An adjacent hall displays portraits of all the Spanish viceroys from Mendoza in 1535 to Juan O'Donojú in 1821.

One of the most significant modern projects was the recovery of the Great Temple, which began in earnest in 1978. The

The now overgrown *Tepanapa*, or Great Temple of Cholula, is the world's largest single-massed man-made structure. A church stands on the platform atop the pyramid on the site of the ancient sanctuaries. Here Cortés averted a massacre by perpetrating one of his own. (©Philip Baird www.anthroarcheart.org)

site had long been known, and once the decision was made, several blocks of colonial buildings of no particular historical or architectural importance were condemned and leveled, to clear the area for excavation. Today the visitor can walk on elevated ramps through the vast ruin, which includes not only the temple itself, but ceremonial halls. Yet this is only a portion of the complex recorded by Cortés and his men; the remainder lies under colonial structures that are themselves deemed irreplaceable monuments and therefore cannot be removed.

In Coyoacán, one may still see the mansion that Cortés built for doña Marina (nearby is the mansion of a more recent female celebrity, Dolores del Rio). A 30-mile drive south of Mexico City leads to Cuernavaca, where Cortés's own mansion now houses the legislative assembly of the State of Morelos. One of the features of this building is a magnificent mural by Diego Rivera, illustrating the history of Morelos, including vivid scenes of the Conquest. The

modern roads do not follow the route of the Cortés expedition, but do lead to many important sites that the Castilians visited en route to the Mexican capital. Cholula is still dominated by the Tepanapa, now overgrown and appearing like a terraced hill surmounted by a Spanish church. Nevertheless, a portion of the complex around its base has been excavated and restored, and the visitor may take a tour of some of the tunnels within the pyramid, showing various stages of its construction. The modern state of Tlaxcala more or less occupies the same area as the old republic that was so essential to Cortés's success. The city of Tlaxcala itself is the state capital, but retains the flavor of a provincial colonial town. Near the coast, in Veracruz state, Cempoala is in ruins, but its remarkable state of preservation requires little imagination to see the Castilians throwing down the idols from the temples.

Perhaps the most poignant site is Tlatelolco, excavated in the early 1960s to become part of a government showpiece known as the "Plaza of the Three Cultures." Immediately south of the broad avenue of San Juan de Letrán is the great temple compound, including the base of the 114 steps described by Bernal Díaz. Indeed, his narrative is so complete that, using his book as a guide, the visitor can still identify many of the ruins. This represents the ancient culture. Immediately behind is the college-convent of Santa Cruz de Tlatelolco, founded in 1536 by Bishop Zumárraga, and representing the colonial culture. Beyond that, devastated by the great earthquake and subsequently rebuilt, are the steel and glass high-rises of the modern culture. To the rear of the temple complex is a stele with the inscription: "On August 13, 1521, after a heroic defense by Cuauhtémoc, Tlatelolco fell to the power of Hernán Cortés. This was neither a triumph nor a defeat, but rather the painful birth of the Mestizo nation that is the Mexico of today."

Glossary of native personalities

The following is a list of native princes and officials who figured prominently in the Conquest. Mexican succession was by *tanastry*, which is to say the throne passed through all the brothers of one generation before going to the next.

Axayacatl (*r.* 1469–81): third emperor and father of the emperors Moctezuma and Cuitláhuac. Cortés was quartered in his palace.

Cacama, King of Texcoco (*r.* 1515–20) (also called Cacamatzin): distant cousin of Moctezuma. His father was the great Texcocoan king and statesman Nezahualpilli (*r.* 1472–1515). Cacama met Cortés en route to Mexico and led him to the city. Died under mysterious circumstances during the *Noche Triste*, probably murdered on Cortés's orders.

Coanacoch (*r.* 1520–21): brother of Cacama, placed on the Texcocoan throne in 1520 after the latter's arrest by Cortés. Reigned one year.

Cualpopoca (*d.* 1520): Mexican governor of the Pánuco and instigator of an uprising against the Castilians on the coast. Burned at the stake toward the end of 1520.

Cuauhtémoc (*c.* 1496–1525) (also called Guatémoc, Guatemotzin): eighth and last emperor. Reigned 1520–21. Son of Ahuítzotl, fifth emperor (*r.* 1486–1502), and a cousin of Moctezuma. Surrendered to Cortés on August 13, 1521. Hanged in Chiapas in 1525, during Cortés's Honduras expedition. Now a national hero and symbol of Mexican resistance to foreign influence.

Cuitláhuac (*d.* 1520): seventh emperor, son of Axayacatl and brother of Moctezuma, whom he succeeded after his deposition. Reigned for a few months until his death of smallpox.

Doña Marina (*c.* 1502–51) native name Malinalli, also known as la Malinche: Indian girl given to the Castilians at Potonchán. Speaking both Chontol Maya and Nahutl, she became Cortés's interpreter and, to a certain extent, confidante, adviser, and spy. She also bore him a son. Married after the Conquest to Juan Jaramillo, she lived quietly on her estates until her death.

Moctezuma (*c.* 1468–1520) correctly Motecuhçoma, also known at Montezuma: sixth emperor of Mexico, and second of that name. Reigned 1502–20. Son of Axayacatl. Deposed and died under mysterious circumstances (probably stoned by a mob) while a prisoner of the Castilians.

Tetlepanquetzal, King of Tacuba (Tlacopán) tortured with Cuauhtémoc.

Teuhtlilli (also called Teudile or Tendile). Mexican diplomat and administrator over the Totonac vassalage, who first met Cortés on the coast. Vanishes from history after Cortés moves into the interior.

Further reading

Primary Sources

For direct quotes from Bernal Díaz del
Castillo's *True History of the Discovery and
Conquest of New Spain*, I have translated from
a Castilian edition published in two volumes
in Mexico City by Editorial Porrua in 1960.
The standard English translation by A.P.
Maudsley was published in two volumes by
the Hakluyt Society in 1908. Maudsley
participated in an excellent abridgement,
supplemented by extracts from Hernan
Cortés's letters, which was published under
the title *The Discovery and Conquest of Mexico*
by Farrar, Straus, Cudahy of New York in
1956. I have used Howard F. Cline's English
translation of Fra Bernardino de Sahagún's
Conquest of New Spain (1585 Revision),
which contains both the Castilian text
and English translation.

Berdan, Frances F., and Patricia Rieff
  Anawalt, eds., *The Essential Codex
  Mendoza*, University of California Press,
  Berkeley, 1997.
Cortés, Hernán, *Letters from Mexico*, trans.
  and ed. by A.R. Pagden, Grossman
  Publishers, New York, 1971.
Díaz del Castillo, Bernal, *Historia Verdadera de
  la Conquista de la Nueva España*, 5th ed.
  Mexico, D.F.: Editorial Porrua, S.A., 1960.
Díaz del Castillo, Bernal, *The Discovery and
  Conquest of Mexico*, trans. by A.P.
  Maudsley, Farrar, Straus, Cudahy, New
  York, 1956.
Durán, Diego (comp),. *The History of the
  Indies of New Spain*, trans. and annot. by
  Doris Heyden. University of Oklahoma
  Press, Norman, 1994.
Fuentes, Patricia, ed. and trans. *The
  Conquistadors: First-person Accounts of the
  Conquest of Mexico*, The Orion Press, New
  York, 1963.
León-Portilla, Miguel, ed. *The Broken Spears:
  The Aztec Account of the Conquest of
  Mexico*, Constable and Company, Ltd.,
  London, 1962.
Sahagún, Bernardino de (comp.), *The
  Conquest of New Spain* (1585 Revision),
  University of Utah Press, Salt Lake
  City, 1989.
Sahagún, Bernardino de (comp.), *Florentine
  Codex: General History of the Things of New
  Spain*, trans. by Arthur J.O. Anderson and
  Charles E. Dibble (12 vols), School of
  American Research, Santa Fe, 1950–82.

Secondary Sources

Atkinson, William C., *A History of Spain and
  Portuga*, Penguin Books Ltd., London, 1960.
Bancroft, Hubert Howe, *History of Mexico.
  Vol. 2*, from *The Works of Hubert Howe
  Bancroft* (39 vols.), A.L. Bancroft & Co.,
  San Francisco, 1883.
Boorstin, Daniel, *The Discoverers*, Random
  House, New York, 1983.
Bridges, Toby, ed. *Black Powder Gun Digest*,
  Follett Publishing Company, Chicago, 1972.
Carrasco, Pedro, *The Tenochca Empire of Ancient
  Mexico: The Triple Alliance of Tenochtitlan,
  Tetzcoco, and Tlacopan.* University of
  Oklahoma Press, Norman, 1999.
Cerwin, Herbert, *Bernal Diaz, Historian of the
  Conquest*, University of Oklahoma Press,
  Norman, 1963.
Chimalpahin Quauhtlehuantzin, Domingo de
  San Antón Muñón, *Codex Chimalpahin:
  Society and Politics in Mexico Tenochtitlan,
  Tlatelolco, Texcoco, Culhaucan, and Other
  Nahua Atlepetl in Central Mexico: The
  Nahuatl and Spanish Annals and Accounts
  Collected and Recorded by don Domingo de San
  Anton Munon Chimalpahin Quauhtlehuantzin*,
  ed. and trans. by Arthur J.O. Anderson and

Susan Schroeder, University of Oklahoma Press, Norman, 1997.

Cypess, Sandra Messinger, *La Malinche in Mexican Literature From History to Myth*, University of Texas Press, Austin, 1991. (Reprinted 2000.)

Hassig, Ross, *Aztec Warfare: Imperial Expansion and Political Control*, University of Oklahoma Press, Norman, 1988. (Reprinted 1995.)

Humble, Richard, et al, *The Explorers*, from *The Seafarers* Series, Time-Life Books, Alexandria, Va.,1978.

Innes, Hammond, *The Conquistadors*, Alfred A. Knopf, New York, 1969.

Kelly, John Eoghan, *Pedro de Alvarado, Conquistador*, Princeton University Press, Princeton, N.J., 1932.

León-Portilla, Miguel, *Bernardino de Sahagún, First Anthropologist*, Mauricio J. Mixco, trans. University of Oklahoma Press, Norman,2002.

López de Gómara, Francisco, *Cortés: The Life of the Conqueror by His Secretary*, University of California Press, Berkeley, 1964.

Miller, Hubert J. Juan de Zumárraga, *First Bishop of Mexico*, Edinburg, Tex., 1973

Miller, Lee, *Roanoke: Solving the Mystery of the Lost Colony*, Penguin Books, New York, 2002.

Prescott, William Hickling, *History of the Conquest of Mexico*, 1843. (Reprinted by the Modern Library, New York, 1998.)

Stewart, Desmond, et al, *The Alhambra*, Newsweek, New York, 1974.

Thomas, Hugh, *Conquest: Montezuma, Cortés, and the Fall of Old Mexico*, Simon & Schuster, New York, 1993.

Time-Life Books, Editors, *Gods of Sun and Sacrifice: Aztec & Maya Myth*, in *Myth and Mankind* Series, Time-Life Books BV, Amsterdam, 1997.

Wood, Michael, *Conquistadors*, University of California Press, Berkeley, 2000.

Wood, Peter et al, *The Spanish Main*, from *The Seafarers* Series, Time-Life Books, Alexandria, Va, 1979.

Articles

Hillerbrand, Hans J., "The Reforming Spirit," Merle Severy, ed., *Great Religions of the World*, National Geographic Society, Washington, 1971.

Kendall, Paul Murray, *"The World of Francis I," The Renaissance, Maker of Modern Man*, National Geographic Society, Washington, 1970.

Index

Visit the Osprey website

- Information about forthcoming books

- Author information

- Read extracts and see sample pages

- Sign up for our free newsletters

- Competitions and prizes

www.ospreypublishing.com